The University of Ulster

Genesis & Growth

Gerard O'Brien
&
Peter Roebuck

EDITORS

FOUR COURTS PRESS

Set in 11pt on 13pt Ehrhardt for
FOUR COURTS PRESS
7 Malpas Street, Dublin 8, Ireland
e-mail: info@fourcourtspress.ie
http://www.fourcourtspress.ie
and in North America for
FOUR COURTS PRESS
c/o ISBS, 920 N.E. 58th Avenue, Suite 300, Portland, OR 97213

ISBN 978–1–84682–139–4

Printed in England
by MPG Books, Bodmin, Cornwall.

Contents

Illustrations

Colour plates occur between pages 82 and 83

Contributors

MIKE CATTO was Senior Lecturer in History and Theory at the University's Belfast Campus. Since his retirement he has worked as a writer and broadcaster. His history of the Belfast Art College is due to be published in 2009.

THOMAS G. FRASER, Emeritus Professor of History, was Provost of the Magee Campus 2002–6. The third edition of his book, *The Arab-Israeli Conflict*, was published by Macmillan in 2007.

ROBERT J. GAVIN, Emeritus Professor of History, was Provost of the Magee Campus and later (1995) Pro-Vice-Chancellor. His forthcoming book on Derry, *Atlantic Gateway*, is to be published by Four Courts Press in 2009.

DON McCLOY was Dean of Science and Technology at the University and (from 1991) Director of the Belfast Institute of Further and Higher Education. His forthcoming history of technical education in Belfast, *Learning to Create*, is due to be published in 2009.

GERARD O'BRIEN is Reader in History at the Magee Campus. His latest book, *An Garda Síochána and the Scott Medal*, was published by Four Courts Press in 2008.

ROSALIND PRITCHARD is Professor of Education and head of the School of Education. She has published extensively on mergers, linkages and federations in London and Welsh universities as well as in relation to those in Northern Ireland.

PETER ROEBUCK, Emeritus Professor of History, was Pro-Vice-Chancellor for Academic Affairs (1992–2000) and Provost of the Coleraine Campus (1992–2006). His most recent book is *The Foundation Decade at Shrigley: Seminary, Church and Shrine, 1929–39* (Rome, 2004).

ARTHUR WILLIAMSON is Professor of Non-Profit Research. Along with an extensive list of publications he is the author of 'The New University of Ulster 1965–84: A Chapter in University-State Relations in Northern Ireland' (PhD, University of Dublin, 1988).

Preface

The formation of the University of Ulster was among the more
seminal developments in higher education in the United Kingdom
and Ireland during the later twentieth century. It involved the merger
of a university and a polytechnic when, hitherto, both types of
institution had been strictly divided by the so-called binary line. The
merger took effect from 1 October 1984 and was so successful that it
is difficult not to regard it as in some sense the herald of the grant of
university status to all polytechnics and many advanced colleges in the
UK in 1992. Thus, as a turning-point leading to a transformation of
the UK higher education sector, the significance of the foundation of
the University was substantial. This book has been written to mark
and celebrate the twenty-fifth anniversary of the merger in 2009.

The origins of the University are explored in the early chapters of
the book, but the roots of the development of Irish scholarship are
long, deep and largely invisible. Perhaps the deepest root of all is the
respect for learning as a value in itself. Early and pre-historic Ulster
had had its share of the schools in which the secular learned class of
Ireland, the *aes dana*, had become proficient at their trade. Later, and
alongside these secular schools, medieval monks established their own
centres of learning. Both types of institution survived for many
centuries the often-violent reversals of fortune which accompanied
changes outside their walls. Even when these places of scholarship and
education themselves became targets and victims, the will to endure
and the urge to build anew, however unpropitious the circumstances,
always re-asserted themselves.

These fundamental qualities survived the advent of fresh demo-
graphic, ethnic and religious developments in early modern times, and
the occurrence of far-reaching political and economic changes in the
nineteenth and early twentieth centuries. By the 1960s Northern
Ireland, separated politically from the rest of the island, but firmly
attached economically, socially and (up to a point) culturally to the
United Kingdom, was ready to take its part in the further development of third-level education which was then becoming a hallmark

of post-war Britain. Once again, as had happened so often in the past in the north of Ireland, the new institutions became embroiled in difficulties. The Lockwood Report which engendered them was fiercely debated. They commenced and continued their work in circumstances which were increasingly subject to violence and disruption. Ultimately, after receipt of the Chilver Report and its rejection by government, they were merged to form the University of Ulster. Continuous change has characterized the experience of the University since then.

The essays which follow have been written by long-serving members of the University of Ulster and of its original constituent bodies, the New University of Ulster and the Ulster Polytechnic. While they constitute a first attempt to place the University in a historical context, the book is not an official history. The University has looked kindly on the project throughout but each of the authors assumes full responsibility for their respective contributions. Each has tried, in very brief compass, to chart the salient points, critical junctures and new departures in the history of the institution. Inevitably, constraints of space have left innumerable avenues unexplored. They have also kept formal scholarly apparatus to a minimum – references are restricted to the sources of direct quotations and of material in the Tables. In addition to being brief, essays have been designed, as far as possible, to be read independently of the whole, as well as in the broadly chronological sequence in which they are placed. The book, and each essay in it, is not only the product of individual authors, but also the outcome of regular consultation, discussion and deliberation amongst the contributors, between the contributors and the editors, and between the editors themselves. It will not be difficult for readers to identify the elements in the University's history where debate has yet to be concluded.

The production of this book has been, in every sense, a collaborative venture. The editors are grateful to the Vice-Chancellor of the University of Ulster, Professor Richard Barnett, for a generous grant-in-aid of publication, and for his assistance throughout the project. Thanks are also due to Library and Graphics staff for assistance in various connections; and especially to Mr Joseph McLaughlin, University Archivist, and his Assistant, Mrs Fiona Clyde, who came to our aid whenever called upon. We are particularly grateful to Mr Patrick Mulvenna of the University's Department of

Corporate Planning and Governance for providing us with the material in the Appendix. On behalf of our fellow contributors, we also wish to thank all those other colleagues, far too numerous to mention, who helped in one way or another with the individual essays, especially those who commented on successive drafts. Armed with copious recommendations, Tony Feenan brought his immense experience to bear on the collation of the illustrations, with expert assistance from Mike Catto and Nigel McDowell. Mrs G.P. Campbell prepared the book for the press with exemplary patience and skill, and did much else besides to keep the venture on track. Finally, it has been a pleasure to work with Martin Fanning and his colleagues at Four Courts Press, and we thank them warmly for the care they took with the final draft.

Perhaps after reading these essays others will set out to do further work on the history, policies, priorities and circumstances of the University of Ulster. That, at least, is our earnest wish.

GERARD O'BRIEN & PETER ROEBUCK

School of History & International Affairs
UNIVERSITY OF ULSTER
April 2008

Antecedents

MIKE CATTO & ROBERT J. GAVIN

'For forms of government let fools contest; Whate'er is best administer'd, is best'.[1]

The history of the University of Ulster and its antecedent institutions is replete with unexpected twists and turns. Geographically, the University's origins are in north-west Ulster, including a temporary link with Dublin. More recent roots were put down in Coleraine and in several old and new institutions in the Belfast area. From 1984 the University flourished on four campuses, in turn linked with regional colleges across Northern Ireland. Academic origins were equally diverse – from Art and Theology in the first instance, to arrays of innovative courses, relatively few of which were identified with traditional academic disciplines. Some course innovation stemmed from research discovery at discipline interfaces; most from student desire to bring relevant theory from various sources to bear upon practice in increasingly sophisticated workplace environments. How students' desires were met, how employers were brought to recognise the value of training for innovation, how teaching teams with the capacity to deliver innovative courses were assembled, deployed and reinforced by research activity, and how the whole enterprise was developed, is what this study is mainly about. The University and its predecessors operated within a regulatory framework that was as often a hindrance as a help. We will discuss government intentions for higher education in the north of Ireland and how they impinged upon University performance. But our main preoccupation will be the University's endeavour to innovate through teaching, research and organisational adaptation in the service of a rapidly changing society.

1 Alexander Pope, *Essay on Man, Epistle Three*, 1734.

THE COLLEGE OF ART

The University's oldest antecedent institution was the College of Art which opened in Belfast in December 1849. Like many other Victorian provincial Art Colleges, it aimed at improving the training of workers and designers in local industries rather than pursuing the Fine Arts. Based in five small rooms rented from Belfast Academical Institution, the first College – or so-called Normal School – was planned as a venture jointly funded by local businessmen and central government. As the former rarely met their obligations, the college risked closure during its first two decades. However, it was successful in producing well-thought-of 'cunning artificers',[2] as one of its headmasters described those who pursued its courses, and by 1900 had established a national reputation for Celtic Revival/Art Nouveau work, especially for the linen and damask industries and the graphical trades. The College of Art twice moved premises before settling in to the York Street building in 1967–8. We will return to that story later.

NINETEENTH-CENTURY MAGEE COLLEGE

We now travel north-west and focus on the cluster of buildings at the top of the twenty-first century Magee campus. The centrepiece is the towered and turreted gothic structure built between 1856 and 1860. The architect, A.P. Gribben of Dublin, deserves as much credit for the building's elegant lines as the College's founders. His instructions were that its façade should be as 'ornamental and imposing' as finance would allow.[3] Otherwise the choice of style was his. The citizens of Derry subscribed half the cost of land and buildings. The rest came from the Honourable the Irish Society, as local landlord, with a small contribution from the Magee trustees. Most of Martha Magee's bequest, that made the venture possible, was invested to provide income to meet recurrent costs. Magee's main building was the scene of practically all the College's academic activity from its opening in 1865 to its last years. The specification called for a common hall for

---

2 Thomas M. Lindsay in his inaugural address as Headmaster, 1870. A full treatment of art and design education and practice in Belfast will be published by Mike Catto shortly.
3 F. Holmes, *Magee College, 1865–1965: the Evolution of the Magee Colleges* (Londonderry, 1965), 25. The other chief study of Magee College is J.R. Leebody, *A Short History of McCrea–Magee College during the First Fifty Years* (Londonderry, 1915).

1 College Avenue, Magee.

500 persons, a library, a museum and four pairs of classrooms, the largest pair seating 150 each. Actual build fell short of this plan. The Great Hall has never seated more than 250. The main building at Queen's University, Belfast, built ten years earlier at nearly quadruple the cost, was twice as large. But Magee had about a quarter of Queen's student numbers and, in various configurations, the main building met Magee's teaching needs for nearly a century.

The red brick buildings along the curve of College Avenue were neither classrooms nor offices until 1950. At the outset Magee's professors had been promised housing. The first two pairs of semi-detached dwellings, funded by a leading shirt manufacturer, William Tillie, and other local donors, were built in 1881–2. Thereafter,

Professor Leebody, a formidable fundraiser, badgered the Irish Society and other funders into completing the College's original plan for a seven-house build. By 1896 the terraced residences extended round from the Northland Road to the main building. The gate lodge building was added in 1911 to accommodate an additional Professor. Carrickmore House, across the Rock Road, was bequeathed in 1915.

Magee's professorial houses were among the finest contemporary residences in Derry. They confirmed the Magee trustees' intent to attract distinguished academic figures. Salaries were competitive with other universities. They attracted men from good academic positions elsewhere and from the Presbyterian ministry. Four Chairs were funded from the £1,000 annual yield from Magee's investments, two others from the endowment gifted in 1858 by Richard Dill, executor of Martha Magee's will and the chief advocate of the University establishment in Derry. The seventh Chair – in Maths and Physics – was financed by an annual grant of £250 from the Irish Society. Salaries were about double those of most Presbyterian ministers. They compared well with the £140 accorded to the next-best-paid educationalists in Derry – the Headmaster and second Master in Foyle College. They were far removed from the £30 stipends of the teachers in the thirty-five or more primary schools in the city. In the nineteenth century teachers at all levels collected fees from pupils and students. Primary pupils paid a penny per week. Magee students paid two guineas per six-month course.

University Professors had other ways of augmenting their incomes. Although Professor of Maths and Physics, Professor Leebody was a Fellow of the Institute of Chemistry; he had his own personal chemistry laboratory when Magee had no laboratory at all. For many years he was public health adviser to Derry Corporation and found his practice as a chemist 'a valuable source of income'.[4] His colleague, Professor Witherow, was a prolific author whose works on church history were widely read but earned him less than his articles in periodicals. For eight years he was also editor of the *Derry Standard* which had one of the largest circulations in Ireland. Other Professors had their own extra-mural activities. On-site residence kept Magee staff present to their students. Professor Leebody hankered after on-site student residence too. But that did not come about until the

---

4 Parliamentary Papers, *Royal Commission on University Education in Ireland*, 1901–3, Minutes of Evidence, Question 7830.

College's final years. Meanwhile, Professorial residence contributed to a sense of collegiality, a hallmark of Magee.

THE NINETEENTH-CENTURY IRISH HIGHER EDUCATION MARKET

The otherwise congenial life of nineteenth-century Magee Professors was disturbed by two major preoccupations – student recruitment and recognition of the College's qualifications. Higher education was expensive: less than one in 200 of the relevant age group could afford it. The favoured few were helped on their way by preparatory schools, for example Foyle College, whose building in 1814 was as large as, and cost more than, Magee College. In 2003 this structure was incorporated into the Magee campus and became the oldest building in the University. The Irish Society invested in Foyle College to combat absenteeism among landlords through enabling their sons to study locally and gain bursaries for entry to Trinity College, Dublin. Trinity College was the goal of other sons of Ireland's wealthier elite with an eye to preparing themselves for leadership roles in society or securing public appointments – an aspiration that Trinity bolstered after 1855 by adjusting its courses to the new civil service examinations. Alternatively, aspiring sons ended up in Oxford or Cambridge, while a scattering went to Scottish universities. Magee could not compete for this kind of entrant. Leavers from preparatory schools like Foyle were not interested in Magee until quite late in the nineteenth century. Ireland's other University Colleges – in Dublin, Belfast, Cork and Galway – were no better placed than Magee to attract the progeny of the Irish landed gentry. They had to look elsewhere for most of their entrants and discover relevant career opportunities for their graduates.

In nineteenth-century Ireland a University degree opened relatively few career opportunities. Most of the employment areas for which the University of Ulster would prepare its students in the late twentieth century either did not exist or were effectively closed to university institutions by employer preference for a different form of training. According to a member of the Council of the Belfast Chamber of Commerce:

it is perfectly impossible to imagine that the system by which so
many businesses, trades and manufactures have been taught for
centuries, will be abandoned at once in favour of a system,
however theoretically perfect, of the results of which no man has
any real practical knowledge whatsoever.[5]

He referred to the system of apprenticeship and the unlikelihood of
its being replaced by, for example, American-style Business Schools.
Whether called by that name or not, apprenticeship of some kind was
practically universal at the time. Whatever level of skill was involved,
training was seen as a dimension of working practice, imparted in the
workplace and evaluated by practitioners. Even the legal, medical,
engineering and teaching professions saw recruitment of personnel in
this light, as did employers in the many trades whose qualifications
were registered after 1889 with the City and Guilds Institute.

At the middle of the nineteenth century some professions
recognised the value of theoretical study. The medical profession had
the liveliest perception of this need and its professional body, the
General Medical Council, formed in 1858, was ready to assign pre-
clinical study to universities and gave limited acceptance to the idea
that universities could compete for clinical instruction with their own
training establishments. Beyond mid-century medical teaching
became the life blood of the University Colleges in Dublin, Belfast,
Cork and Galway, accounting for well over half their students. The
legal and engineering professions in Ireland were less enamoured of
such assistance and made much smaller demands on universities.
Agriculture did not seek university help until the twentieth century
and Queen's premature entry into the field in Belfast came to grief.
One reason why Irish universities failed to expand in the nineteenth
century was society's tardy acceptance of the notion that they had a
role to play in preparing young people for the world of work.

Except for Trinity College they were also largely excluded by
employer fiat and government regulation from the professional area
most suited to the scholarship and theoretical study in which they
excelled. At mid-century about two-thirds of Oxford graduates
entered the church. Preparation for the ecclesiastical ministry was a
rich field for University work elsewhere in the United Kingdom.

---

5 Parliamentary Papers, *Royal Commission on University Education in Ireland*, 1901–3,
Minutes of Evidence, Question 7598.

There was a healthy demand for graduates and universities had considerable power over appointments. Up to 1869 Trinity College disposed of nearly 500 advowsons or rights to present ministers to parishes. Oxford and Cambridge Colleges were similarly endowed and on occasion used these livings to enable outstanding but married alumni, like Thomas Malthus, to continue their research. Trinity College had privileged access in Ireland to parish appointments by the established church. But, unlike its English counterpart, the Church of Ireland served only a small minority of the Irish population. Training for the more than 2,000-strong Catholic priesthood was provided exclusively in Catholic seminaries at home and abroad. There were some 700 students in these seminaries – a somewhat larger number than the entire student population of the three Queen's Colleges at mid-century. As the Catholic Church handled the whole process of training from recruitment to placement, Irish universities were kept out of the picture. In any case, Government decided in 1849 that it would not endow denominational education. The Queen's Colleges could only offer their first years of Arts study to those wishing to enter the Protestant ministry. Nevertheless, the largest single group of students at Queen's Belfast at mid-century intended entering the Presbyterian ministry. To do so they had to complete their theological studies elsewhere. Religious controversy fragmented the higher education market and kept nineteenth-century Irish universities small.

Yet, religious controversy also created a temporary gap in higher education provision that enabled Magee College to compete with other institutions. In normal circumstances Derry would have stood little chance of becoming a seat of learning. In 1845, when Prime Minister Peel proposed to establish 'provincial colleges' in Ireland, merchants and ship owners, ecclesiastics and office holders in Derry gathered and charged their two Parliamentary representatives with pressing the city's claims. Despite their enthusiasm, they had little hope of success. However, four years earlier, the Presbyterian Assembly in Ireland had become so disturbed by the alleged prevalence of Unitarian tendencies among staff of the Belfast Academical Institution that they had withdrawn recognition of its certificate as a qualification for entry to the Presbyterian ministry. Seeking an alternative, the Assembly issued an appeal for the establishment of a Presbyterian training institution that could guarantee the orthodoxy of its staff. Martha Magee in Dublin answered that call. Over the following eight years she and the executors of her will vigorously

2 The earliest known photograph of Magee College, *c.* 1865–70.

pursued the projected creation of a Presbyterian Arts and Theology College in Derry, well away from the Belfast maelstrom. The transfer of higher education from the offending Academical Institution to the new Queen's College, Belfast in 1849, and the Assembly's creation of its own Theological College in Belfast in 1853, ended the dispute between the church and Belfast academia. But by then commitments had been made and court judgements delivered that led inexorably toward the establishment of the College in Derry and its recognition as an appropriate educator of Presbyterian ministers.

RECRUITMENT AND PLACEMENT OF FULL-TIME STUDENTS

Magee's opportunistic origins told against it in its early years. The Presbyterian Church's annual requirement for between twenty and thirty new ministers entailed an enrolment of about 200, respectable for a University College at the time and more than justifying Magee's complement of seven staff. The first two years' intakes of twenty-six and twenty-two students were promising. But then problems arose. The College had to compete for entrants to its Arts courses against the Queen's Colleges in Belfast, Galway and Cork, which disposed of state bursaries. Students paid their way through College, hoping to win prizes or scholarships to assist them. Three-quarters or more of Magee's entrants came from among farmer's sons scattered across the north and west of Ireland from Ballymoney to Letterkenny. Until the last two decades of the century, when the new intermediate schools came into the picture, most received the classical education required for entry from Presbyterian ministers in the parishes. Even the entrants from Derry, always quite a small minority, came mostly from the rural parishes in the vicinity rather than from the city. The rural north-west remained Magee's chief recruitment ground until the century's end when more began to come from other parts of Ulster. Magee students needed aid that the College initially did not have. After the first flush, applications for entry declined.

Those who graduated from Magee's theology courses faced sharp competition when they applied for posts. The government-endowed Assembly's College with its handsome scholarships had almost twice as many entrants as Magee during Magee's first ten years. Thereafter the proportion shifted until Magee received more male entrants than

3 The Great Hall, Magee.

the Belfast College from 1905 onwards, though the latter remained a powerful competitor. In addition a small number of those intent on entering the ministry in Ireland still followed the traditional route to Glasgow and Edinburgh Universities, whither practically all aspirants had gone up to 1810 (the main Magee building was built of Scottish freestone in commemoration). Faced with such competition, on average fewer than seven of Magee College's graduates in the years between 1870 and 1910 took up vacancies in the Presbyterian Church in Ireland – less than a third of the available appointments.

Not all Magee College students graduated in divinity and not all those who qualified as pastors entered the ministry in Ireland. From 1870 onwards Magee students regularly took pastoral posts in Scotland and England. The largest alternative outlet, however, was overseas. In the College's first twenty years no less than 17 per cent of its entrants found careers abroad; 60 per cent of these followed a well-worn path from Derry to the United States and Canada, where most served as pastors while a few others entered education or business. Emigration diminished in the following twenty-five years. Fewer went to North America. No post-1895 College entrants went to Australia, New Zealand or Southern Africa – previously quite popular destinations. More went instead to China, India and the Middle East as missionaries, doctors or teachers.

PART-TIME AND WOMEN STUDENTS

For its first fifteen years Magee could not award degrees. It counted on the Presbyterian Assembly's recognition of the Magee certificate as degree-equivalent. This covered theological study only and offered little comfort to those involved with Arts courses. Hopes of university affiliation were dashed in 1866 and 1873 when relevant initiatives came to nought. Magee intakes slumped after both these disappointments. Lower enrolments meant smaller fee income. In 1868 student entry dropped from eighteen to ten and in the following five years averaged between five and six. In the winter of 1868 Professor Leebody began offering programmes of twenty-five lectures in Physics and Chemistry to the general public, while another Professor offered similar programmes in English literature. Between twenty and thirty students attended these courses which were made available over the following seven years. In 1877 Leebody resumed his scientific programmes on a new basis with nominal fees, having persuaded the Irish Society to endow them. At that the whole project took off in one of those popular educational surges that occurred from time to time in nineteenth-century Ireland. Leebody's first set of twenty-five lectures on Physics attracted 130 subscribers and must have taxed the capacity of Magee's Great Hall. In the following year two separate courses on Physics and Chemistry were offered, with seventy-six and eighty-seven enrolments respectively. These continued annually until 1890 with attendances varying between sixty and ninety-seven. In the 1890s more advanced programmes attracted smaller groups, averaging fifty-seven students, studying for degree-level examinations and forerunners of the future national certificates. On a rough estimate, about half of Magee's full-time equivalent students were part-time between 1877 and 1881, around 20 per cent throughout the 1880s, and 15 per cent in the 1890s.

Half of Leebody's extra-mural students were women. This led on naturally to undergraduate courses for women once Magee College itself was authorised to enter students for university examinations. The formation of the Royal University of Ireland in 1879 made this possible. It incorporated the three Queen's Colleges in Belfast, Galway and Cork along with the Catholic University College in Dublin. It also included Magee College and, like the University of London, allowed students of both genders to prepare externally for its degrees. Magee's Arts Faculty got a fellowship post, membership of the University's

Senate and participation in its examinations process. Ahead of other
Colleges, Magee opened its lectures and scholarships to women. In
Dublin and Belfast Intermediate Schools took the lead in preparing
women for Royal University examinations. In Derry Magee College
partnered the Victoria High School, run by the Magee-trained McKillip
sisters, in enabling women to pass matriculation examinations and
complete undergraduate courses. Leebody secured scholarships for
women from the Irish Society and London Companies for degree
study at Cambridge and London as well as through the Royal
University. Up to 1899 more women attended university courses at
Magee than at Queen's, Belfast, which itself was far ahead of other
Irish universities in this respect. Most Magee women students initially
came from Derry but within a few years its reputation spread and
women of all denominations came from England and India, Belfast
and Dublin, Tuam and Limerick, Wicklow and Wexford. In the first
two decades of the twentieth century 40 per cent of Magee's entrants
were women. Women entrants enabled Magee to maintain its overall
student numbers in the last two decades of the nineteenth century
when Trinity and the University Colleges in Ireland were alarmed by
their declining enrolments.[6]

Gender of Magee entrants, 1865–1921

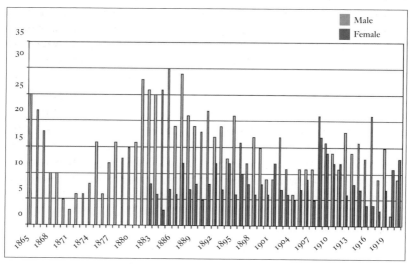

6 Table compiled from J. Leebody, *A Short History of McCrae–Magee College during its
First Fifty years* (1915), 40–83; Magee College Calendars, 1907–23.

A SHIFT TO SCIENCE BAULKED BY PARTITION

Magee was much weakened by the 1908 dissolution of the liberal, open-door, all-Ireland, Royal University of Ireland that had enabled it and Women's Colleges to flourish. In its place, Dublin, Cork and Galway were united in a single University in the south and Queen's, Belfast became an independent university in the north. Magee was left out. Hints were dropped that it might affiliate with Queen's. But the Magee President, Leebody, was sceptical. He opposed the dissolution of the Royal University, doubted the independent viability of Queen's, Belfast with its 300 students, and was unconvinced of the Belfast institution's willingness to agree an affiliation arrangement. Instead he did a deal with the prestigious Trinity College, Dublin whereby Magee students would, on meeting a brief residence requirement, be eligible for the award of Trinity degrees and prizes. Magee's theology students were separately covered by the Royal Charter of 1881 which recognised divinity degrees awarded by the joint theological Faculties of Magee College and the Assembly's College in Belfast.

Leebody believed that he had the means to transform Magee. His close friend Basil McCrea was one of the most dynamic businessmen in the North-West, having made a fortune in transport. With his associate, John McFarland, he sold the idea of light railways as the key to progress in Ireland's western counties and they became owners of the Londonderry and Lough Swilly railway and much else besides. McCrea sympathised with Leebody's ideas for the development of science teaching at Magee. In 1905 he endowed a new Chair in Chemistry, financed a Physics laboratory and in 1907 left his whole estate worth some £70,000 to Magee for College development (subject to the life interest of his sister, who died in 1920). McCrea's estate was worth more than all Magee's previous endowments and in 1911 the College was re-named the McCrea-Magee College. Leebody planned to increase Magee's Arts Professors from five to nine, with two more in science, and two in languages, plus teaching assistants. He proposed to build additional laboratories, student residences and playing fields. Had his scheme been carried through, Magee would have met the challenges of the time.

In the first years of the twentieth century Ireland began to realise that advanced technical, scientific and business education were the keys to industrial progress, that the United Kingdom was falling behind Germany and the United States, and that major new investment in education was required. The same perceptions that drove Leebody prompted the Belfast municipality to establish its Technical Institute/College of Technology in 1901, the first of whose permanently staffed schools was the School of Art, which had been nurtured for thirty years by the Department of Science and Art in South Kensington while being housed in the Belfast Academical Institution. Other specialist areas of work in engineering, domestic science and business were established at the Belfast College of Technology in the first decade of the twentieth century. Some later became the seedlings from which the Polytechnic and the University of Ulster grew.

Within a decade Leebody's hopes of developing science in the north-west were dashed by the effects of war and partition. Wartime inflation ruined the finances of Magee and the Assembly's College, along with others reliant on fixed incomes. In 1922 two of Magee's three theology Professors went to Belfast to help both institutions survive. When the College received the McCrea bequest in 1920, only £1,000 of an expected £3,000 annual income was realisable. The rest was in Lough Swilly Railway shares which Irish partition and other factors rendered practically worthless. Financial stringency stopped the College in its tracks. Far from making a shift to science, the existing science laboratory became a common room. The College was confined to Arts teaching. While other universities in Ireland grew slowly between the wars, Magee went backwards. With only one theology Professor, Magee divinity students completed most of their studies elsewhere, notably at the Assembly's College in Belfast. Magee entrants outnumbered other entrants to that College in sixteen of the twenty years between 1926 and 1945. As fewer entrants to the ministry came by other routes, Magee became by default the chief provider of Northern Ireland's Presbyterian clergy. Nineteenth-century Magee graduates had been a minority in the Northern Ireland Presbyterian ministry. In the twentieth century they were a majority and Magee alumni became a powerful lobby.[7]

7 Table compiled from R. Allen, *The Presbyterian College, Belfast, 1853–1953* (Belfast, 1954), 344–7; Northern Ireland House of Commons Papers, *Report on the possible development of Magee College* [Cmd 275] (Belfast, 1950), table 2.

Students exiting Magee for theological study: students entering
Assembly's College Belfast, 1926–45

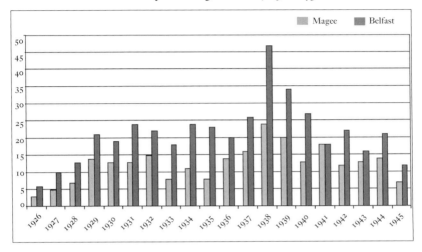

WARTIME AND POST-WAR MAGEE

In 1940 Magee's buildings became the local military headquarters
from which the battle of the Atlantic was fought. They looked down
upon the ship repair yards and berthing for the Royal Navy's largest
concentration of warships. Wartime Derry was an exceptionally
powerful naval base – but was dismantled at the war's end as hastily as
it had been constructed. Among the demolished buildings was a set of
wooden huts immediately above the present car park at Magee. These
concealed a large subterranean plotting table for monitoring the
movements of convoys and their escorts. It replicated a similar
installation in Liverpool where strategy was determined. The facility
at Magee was chiefly used for anti-submarine training and laid the
basis for the post-war HMS *Sea Eagle* training centre. Professors were
ousted from their dwellings for the duration and Magee students
followed their courses in the Model School.

The College recovered slowly from the war. Its staff were under-
paid and overworked as they sought to offer a broad range of courses
for limited numbers of students with inadequate resources. In 1938
the College had received a small subvention from government. In
1950 it still relied on its endowments for 70 percent of its income.

4 Dill House, Magee, student residence and wartime naval headquarters
during the Battle of the Atlantic.

Government grants defrayed more than half United Kingdom universities' expenditures and nearly 60 per cent of Queens' costs. Magee received but 15 per cent of its income from government. Since 1920 government had argued that Magee prepared for the degrees of an institution (Trinity College, Dublin) that lay outside its jurisdiction and offered a denominational education that government could not support. The College sought to overcome the latter difficulty by designating two College Avenue houses as the abode of 'Magee Theological College'. This opened the way to appropriate legislation in 1953 and normal government funding of the remaining 'Magee University College' housed in the other buildings. Increased student numbers and staff removed previous teaching diseconomies and allowed the establishment of new specialisms. Magee began to participate in the wave of educational expansion that marked this period in Northern Ireland. A re-vitalised College was in full flood of development, planning new courses and areas of activity when the Lockwood Committee for the review of higher education in Northern Ireland met in 1965.

THE COLLEGE OF ART COMES OF AGE

The same may be said of the College of Art, which came of age in the decade prior to Lockwood's appointment. During the previous half century the College had occupied the top floor of the Belfast College of Technology with its common studios, specialist workshops and excellent light conditions. The curriculum changed modestly as the century progressed. Until the late 1950s students still undertook a very broad art, design and craft education before venturing upon specialisation in the last of their four years. The first moves to alter the status and character of the College were made in 1933. The then Headmaster, Ivor Beaumont, pressed the City Corporation and Department of Education to set up a College of Art and Design, which would be both separate from the rest of the 'Tech', and would formally recognise its role as the regional art college for all six counties as well as for Belfast. Beaumont's successor, James Warwick, the first alumnus of the college to be appointed its Headmaster/Principal, saw this campaign through to fruition. In the late 1950s the College was re-named the Ulster College of Art and Design. It became the only art college in the UK to be funded by central rather than local government, apart from the postgraduate-only Royal College of Art in London. This central funding enabled the construction of a new building in York Street, occupied in 1967–8. There, Art and Design studies survived the Polytechnic's centralising urges to become the Belfast campus of the University of Ulster. In popular parlance the York Street building remains the 'College of Art'. Central funding and the independent status accorded the 'Ulster College of Art and Design' also facilitated the pursuit of recognition for the College's diplomas in the then rather uncertain field of Art and Design higher-level qualifications. The new Ulster College of Art and Design's degree-equivalent aspirations and general dynamism earned it separate consideration and treatment by the Lockwood Committee.

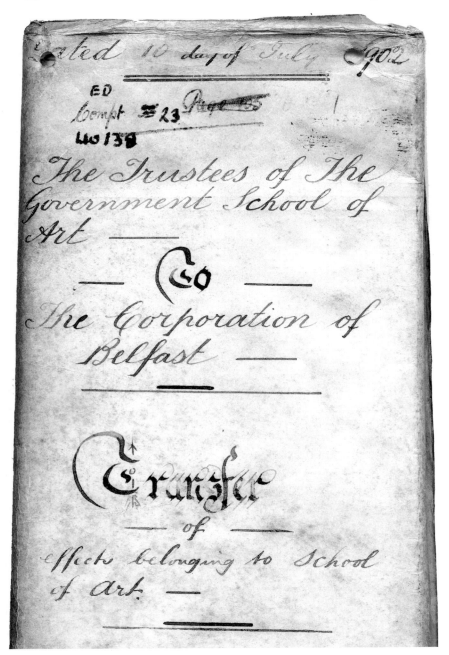

Dated 10 day of July 1902

ED
Compt ≡ 23 Page
40 138

The Trustees of The Government School of Art ——

—— & To ——

The Corporation of Belfast ——

Transfer —— of —— effects belonging to School of Art. ——

5 Deed of Transfer of the Government School of Art, Belfast, to Belfast Corporation, 1902.

POST-WAR FLOWERING OF SPECIALIST COLLEGES

The College of Domestic Science also attracted Lockwood's attention. The key role it had played in promoting women's training at Belfast's Institute/College of Technology led to government giving it responsibility for training Domestic Science teachers to avoid sending trainee teachers to English colleges. By 1933 it had turned the tables and was supplying Britain as well as Northern Ireland and branching out into the training of institutional housekeepers. In 1945 it launched a Certificate course in Institutional Management. These higher-level, full-time programmes were backed up by a range of evening classes in the catering, household economy and institutional management fields for more than 1,000 students. In 1962 the space-hungry 'Tech' was glad to see the Domestic Science College move to its own site at Garnerville on the eastern outskirts of Belfast.

Garnerville's and the Art College's traditions reached far into the past, as did those of Magee College. But all these players on Northern Ireland's higher education scene took on a new life in the two decades after the 1947 Education Act offered a new deal for secondary and further education. Numbers swelled, roles altered, prospects were transformed. Higher education scenery changed as Queen's University expanded, the 'Tech' burst its seams and government proposed to set up autonomous Colleges of Music and of Commerce, as well as founding a Physical Education College at Jordanstown in 1953 to meet specialist teacher-training needs. In 1954 the common workshops and laboratories for engineering, shared between Queen's and the 'Tech' since the first decade of the century, were re-equipped and re-housed in the Ashby Building next to Queen's and given special status under a 'Joint Authority'. By the 1950s new institutions and new traditions were being created almost by the day and some in government were determined to call a halt. A number of the new creations did not survive Lockwood.

THE GROWING 'HIDDEN ECONOMY' OF UNRECOGNISED HIGHER EDUCATION

Meanwhile a less tangible tradition was burgeoning, hardly noticed by Lockwood but which was to have a major influence on the course of higher education. The tradition of personal advancement through continuing education had become particularly strong in Northern

Ireland and was developing portentous ramifications. Leebody's evening classes had been an early manifestation, corresponding to contemporary developments in mechanics institutes throughout the UK. It was bolstered in the early twentieth century by the expansion of technical education in colleges like the Belfast College of Technology. These gradually supplemented or supplanted training provided through the apprenticeship system that decayed faster in Northern Ireland than elsewhere – by 1962 only 14 per cent of Northern Ireland school leavers entered apprenticeships compared with 38 per cent in Great Britain. By then, whole sectors, like retailing, had no apprentices. Others, like textiles and clothing, provided little more than peer induction into in-house industrial practices. Growing bureaucracies recruited well-schooled clerks, about 10 per cent of whom spent an average hour-and-a-half per week at evening classes. Some learned basic office skills. Others took professional examinations up to and including the Queen's degree in Commerce, exceptionally opened to evening class students in 1915. All was done with minimal employer support. Apprenticeship arrangements were tighter in engineering and the well-organised printing trade. But evening classes in science and maths, technical and crafts areas were as popular as those in commerce. For those workers, too, the evening class was the main pathway to broadening one's skill base, deepening one's knowledge and preparing for professional examinations.

Evening classes were taken in the employee's rather than the employer's time. After 1947 government sought to lighten the workers' burdens by abolishing fees and pressing employers to accord their workers day-release. Northern Ireland employers proved less forthcoming than their British counterparts. However, there was another side to this picture. Self-reliant workers gained a certain sense of freedom and control over their own destinies. Particularly in Northern Ireland, where many believed that who you knew counted for more than what you knew, self-training seemed to offer an opportunity to take control of one's own destiny. This may partly explain the enthusiasm for evening classes in which between 20,000 and 25,000 regularly participated across most of the period between 1920 and 1970.

Student enthusiasm for part-time study was shared by teachers in the various technical colleges across Northern Ireland. In the 1950s

6 The original buildings of Magee College, constructed 1856–61.

few of them had degrees, fewer still had teacher's qualifications. Most had Higher Certificates and memberships of professional institutes gained through part time study but as important were their claims to work experience. The majority taught part-time while practising professionally. Full-time staff came from the ranks of the part-timers – another demonstration of advancement through part-time participation. This body of staff was familiar with the peculiarly British mixed economy of industrial training – its shifting fudges and compromises, anachronisms, disparities and discontinuities. Linking theory with practice was second nature to them. They understood the differing teaching modes from evening work to various forms of block release and work-based placement. Most had climbed ladders of opportunity that led from certificates to diplomas and degrees and could differentiate rungs above from those below. They had a wary perception of the power of professional and other validating bodies. In the post-war years, they sensed the quickening pace of change. In pre-war days annual national certificate passes numbered less than twenty. In 1946 ninety-seven passed at ordinary and forty-six at higher level. Sixteen years later both these figures had trebled. Colleges' certificate holders multiplied faster than university graduates. Training was shifting from industry to Colleges. Above all, the quality of training required was moving ever upwards. Pre-war scientific discoveries gave way to post-war accelerating technological advance. In 1950 Northern Ireland industrialists worried chiefly about the quality of machine room skills. In that year the numerically controlled machine tool first appeared. Its development transformed the machine room and much else besides. The teachers of advanced technical courses could sense this wind of change. Having climbed their several difficult paths, they were equipped to scale the new heights that loomed before them. They awaited a banner to lead them forward.

2

Lockwood and After

GERARD O'BRIEN *writes more vividly*

'It is good to know that some people regarded us as naïve, incompetent and ignorant and that there is some gross disadvantage in being English'.[1]

THE BACKDROP

The decision to establish a second university in Northern Ireland had roots that were political as well as social and educational. Any account, therefore, of the origins of the New University of Ulster and the Ulster Polytechnic would be incomplete, not to say baffling, unless due consideration is given to each of these elements. Moreover, each element naturally has an historical context, and it is with these interwoven contexts that our story, if it is to make sense, should best begin.

The political atmosphere in which the desirability of new third-level institutions was thought about, discussed and decided upon in Northern Ireland during the early 1960s was not without its tensions. Since the mid-1950s the state had been the target of an armed campaign by a small but determined coterie of the Irish Republican Army which aimed to terminate the constitutional connection between Northern Ireland and the United Kingdom. The IRA was acting independently of the government of the Republic of Ireland, though since the separation of the two jurisdictions in the early 1920s successive administrations in Dublin, of whichever party, had placed re-unification at the top of the national political wish-list.

Times of course had changed since the wild days of the 1920s. The two states had for many years rubbed along together without

---

1 Imperial College, London, Sir Willis Jackson Papers, Sir John Lockwood to Sir Willis Jackson, 4 March 1965.

disharmony in mundane spheres such as postal facilities, customs and excise, and day-to-day legalities. The Garda Síochána and the Royal Ulster Constabulary worked together quietly to ensure that lawlessness did not prosper in border areas. Also, whereas veteran politicians of the 1920s continued to hold cabinet office in the Republic even into the 1960s, they were at last being forced to make room for younger men with less time-locked attitudes. While official visits to Belfast by southern ministers had to wait until 1965, unofficial visits (even by Eamon de Valera himself) could be arranged through a single phone call. When the IRA campaign was forced to a halt in 1962 this was due in part to the co-operation of the Dublin government. The psychological legacy for the Unionist people of Northern Ireland, however, of such a lengthy and sustained assault on their state by a traditional enemy, while difficult to measure, could not have been other than very considerable. The ever-uneasy relations between those Unionists and the Nationalists who were believed to be collectively 'in the state but not of it' likewise could only have worsened.

In the educational sphere partition had brought very mixed blessings to Northern Ireland. Despite several attempts to rationalise the complex school system inherited from the pre-1920 all-Ireland regime, old entrenchments largely prevailed, and the schools of Ulster remained a political and sectarian battleground long after the intensity of such sentiments had faded in less contentious areas of society. But in third-level institutions the picture was somewhat brighter. By the 1930s Queen's University felt able to recognise Irish history formally as a legitimate subject. Academic and intellectual societies operated on a cross-border basis. Notwithstanding the armed strife of the 1916–23 period and the thickening atmosphere of 'faith and fatherland' which was to follow, Londonderry's Magee College managed to sustain its relationship with Dublin's Trinity College. As part of an arrangement dating from 1909 Trinity students spent the latter part of their undergraduate careers at Magee.

But despite the persistent shadows of the past, the bright new educational world of post-World War II promised much for Northern Ireland as it did for the rest of the United Kingdom. The period of the 'baby boom' encompassed also the coming of universal secondary schooling, a rise in affluence, and the introduction of financial support for students. In the years before the war, and for a short time after, many students still lived at home; the arrival of student grants meant that it was now possible for students to study outside their home area.

The primary implications, both short- and long-term, were that student numbers were set to grow and that more and more resources in terms of buildings and facilities were going to be needed. By the time the British government got round to establishing the Robbins Committee at the beginning of the 1960s to take the third-level pulse of the nation and recommend accordingly, events had already overtaken the policy-makers and there was little for Robbins to do but 'legitimise what had by then become inevitable'.[2]

THIRD-LEVEL PROBLEMS IN POST-WAR
NORTHERN IRELAND

These implications were not lost on the civil servants of Stormont, the business entrepreneurs of Ulster generally, and perhaps more particularly on the staff, students and graduates of Magee College. The demand for places in higher education had been rising for some years and it was becoming clear that soon Queen's University would not be able to meet it. The region's one university, a former Queen's College opened in the 1840s, would simply run out of space. Built originally on what had once been the edge of the town of Belfast, Queen's was now on the edge of Belfast City centre where building land was at a premium and where the very awareness of the University's predicament would push the prices even higher. It was of course open to the Stormont government merely to take no action or initiative and thereby quietly export Ulster's overspill to mainland universities. But within months of the setting-up of the Robbins Committee in February 1961 the Northern Ireland Ministry of Education began to come under pressure, not only from Magee College but also from the Armagh County Education Committee. The economic as well as the social benefits of establishing a new university within Ulster could not be evaded or denied; local interest would simply be too strong. The founding of just such a new university was, therefore, largely a foregone conclusion. Of course, Queen's and Magee were not the region's only third-level institutions: the Ulster College of Art and Design had opened its doors in 1849, and the Belfast College of Technology in 1907. As the university issue came under consideration at Stormont in the early 1960s, the College of Domestic Science

2 Roy Lowe, *Education in the Post-War Years: A Social History* (New York, 1988), 172.

moved out of the 'Tech' premises to its own site near Belfast. Also on
the edge of Belfast was the Ulster College of Physical Education.

What was less than clear at the start was whose responsibility the
initiative should be, as regards a possible new university. By the very
nature of the Government of Ireland Act 1920 under which the state
had been established, Northern Ireland was the most 'self-governing'
of the United Kingdom's several regions. However, the principal
limitation within that arrangement was, crucially, fiscal: Stormont was
dependent on permission from the Treasury in London for any
unusual proposed expenditure. Also, in the present instance, a
mainland-based committee was up and running under Lord Robbins
on the whole question of British higher education and its future.
Robbins had been tasked 'to review the pattern of full-time higher
education in Great Britain.'[3] Northern Ireland had not been
mentioned specifically, but then nor had Wales or Scotland. In the
event Robbins extended his inquiries to cover Wales and Scotland but
not Northern Ireland. When the Stormont civil servants broached the
matter directly with the Treasury in the summer of 1961, six months
after Robbins had set to work, they were told it was now too late to
insert Northern Ireland into the committee's crowded agenda. The
question as to why the Stormont administrators delayed their
approach until the Robbins Committee was well under way is still an
open one; but if (as one suspects) it was done in the hope that future
developments would be under the closer control of Stormont rather
than London, then that is what transpired, though the problematic
end result could scarcely have been foreseen at the outset. It is worth
pointing out, however, that the decision not to include Ulster in the
committee's deliberations seems to have been made outside Northern
Ireland and at the beginning of the work.

THE STORMONT OFFICIALS AND THE UGC

The ministry lost no time thereafter, though, in taking soundings from
the University Grants Committee (UGC) as to whether Robbins's
eventual recommendations might be adaptable or at least helpful in
deciding matters in Northern Ireland. But unsurprisingly it was too

---

3 *Higher Education: Report of the Committee appointed by the Prime Minister under the
Chairmanship of Lord Robbins, 1961–63* (London, 1963), 1.

early for the UGC to read such entrails or to commit itself to any possible point of view. By the beginning of 1962 it was clear to the Stormont administrators that they were on their own in the matter and that a wait-and-see approach would be irresponsible. In mid-February (as Northern Ireland government records indicate) it was decided that the future of the university 'question' in Northern Ireland would be dealt with by the region's own government. The early approaches from Derry and Armagh (as well as one from Coleraine) were kept firmly at bay while the ministry considered its strategy. An important early aspect of the game-plan was to discourage the clinging attentions of the UGC. The UGC had responded with irritating vagueness the previous year when the men from Belfast had sought advice on policy. Now, having moved the responsibility into the Belfastmen's court, the UGC was very willing to furnish any amount of advice on where Ulster's new university ought to be sited. For the rest of 1962 the men in London were fed incomplete, inaccurate and generally worthless statistical data by the Belfastmen, until the penny dropped and the UGC withdrew its offer of 'advice' with ill-concealed fury.

A week before the UGC withdrew in dudgeon senior civil servants in Belfast decided to establish 'a local committee to consider Higher Education, including the need for a second university'. To set the stage for such a committee and to provide it with necessary guidance and information a working party was planned, to be made up of officials from the ministries of Labour, Commerce, Education and Finance. While these wheels were being put in motion senior officials from Belfast's Ministry of Finance met with Sir Keith Murray, Chairman of the UGC, to tell him reproachfully of their 'disappointment' at his committee's response to their statistics and to seek his blessing for their proposed local committee. Murray smiled on the proposal and offered the oblique suggestion that the Ulster officials might find it useful to pack their proposed committee with English academics rather than with local representatives. On the previous day officials from Belfast's Ministry of Education had had an infinitely more fruitful meeting with P.S. Ross, secretary to the Robbins Committee. At this meeting Ross undertook to provide the Stormont government from that moment forward with all papers and statistical tables used by his Committee, along with the Committee's draft report. He also gave them 'in confidence the conclusions already reached or likely to be reached by his Committee'. More importantly Ross, a Treasury official with the benefit of two years' experience of Robbins behind him, cautioned the Belfast officials against wasting time and resources by seeking to repeat Robbins's performancé in an Ulster setting. Instead, he suggested, they should establish 'a small committee which could listen to the views of outside parties and make a report on how "Robbins" should be adapted for Northern Ireland'.[4] The Robbins Report was due for publication in October 1963, a mere nine months away at the time of the meeting with Ross. As long as the proposed inter-ministerial working party did its duty efficiently and the new committee was well furnished with data, the work could be brought to a conclusion quite quickly.

THE FORMATION OF THE LOCKWOOD COMMITTEE

The working party began to meet from early March 1963. Its existence was deliberately kept secret, and requests to outside agencies for data and information were conducted through individual members of the party under letterheads from their various ministries. By May enough preparations had been made for the administration to consider the membership of the proposed Committee and to start looking for a Chairperson. The members, it was felt, should be of an Ulster background and, while not actually involved in higher education in Northern Ireland, have some knowledge of university administration. The search for a Chairperson ran aground at an early stage when, having wasted an entire summer in fruitless negotiations, the government's first choice, Sir William Iliff, ex-civil servant, impeccable Ulsterman and leading international banker, turned down the offer. The officials began to broader the parameters of their search. To preserve the Committee's independence and integrity it was felt undesirable that either the Chairperson or any Committee-member should be a serving member of Robbins or the UGC. The Chairperson preferably should have some familiarity with Ulster, be experienced in establishing new universities, and be able to work to a fairly tight deadline. Sir John Lockwood, former Vice-Chancellor of the University of London, with vast experience of setting up new universities in far-flung corners of the world, was first suggested by

4 Quotes in this paragraph are from: Public Record Office of Northern Ireland, FIN 18/41/8.

the Ministry of Education in London. The suggestion received perhaps crucial local endorsement from W.T. Ewing of the NI Ministry of Education who had seen Lockwood in action when the latter had chaired the Secondary Schools Education Council, and had formed a high opinion of his chairmanship abilities. By early October Lockwood had accepted the chairmanship of the committee (his last, as it turned out) which was to see his name pass into history in a manner he could not have foreseen.

As the publication date of the Robbins Report approached the Stormont officials bent their attention to an increasingly frantic search for acceptable (and willing) members to people the proposed Committee. Ross's successor as secretary of the Robbins Committee, a Mr Gerrard, put forward the name of Sir Willis Jackson, Professor of Electrical Engineering at London's Imperial College of Science and Technology and a man of formidable committee experience in the field of technical education. The London Ministry of Education had suggested also Sir Peter Venables, Principal of Birmingham's College of Advanced Technology, an inveterate committee man who had once been shortlisted for membership of the Robbins Committee. On that same shortlist at one time, and also recommended to the Northern Ireland government by Gerrard, was Miss A.R. Murray, tutor-in charge of New Hall, Cambridge. Miss Murray was Vice-President of the British Federation of Business and Professional Women and had been stationed in Derry as Chief Officer of the WRNS during the Second World War. On Lockwood's Committee she was to be the token female who would offset the otherwise all-male make-up of the group. All these 'mainlanders' were acceptable to the Stormont administrators, despite the fact that they would make up half of the committee, not forgetting the fact that as Chairman Lockwood would also have a casting vote. That the Committee was structured in this way reflected the government's intention merely to adapt Robbins's recommendations to an Ulster environment instead of staging a re-run of the entire Robbins exercise in microcosm. It was decided, therefore, to 'resist any suggestion that every possible interest in Northern Ireland has to be represented on the Committee'.[5]

For the remaining 'half' of the committee the government looked to those local interests with penetrating selectivity. A grammar school headmaster and an industrialist were identified, William Mol of

5 PRONI, FIN 58/12.

Ballymena Academy who was also President of the Ulster Headmasters'
Association, and Dr Denis Rebbeck, Managing Director of Harland
and Wolff. Both agreed to serve, but delays caused by the odd refusal
– the government failed to find a suitable 'man in the street'
(preferably a Roman Catholic) – led to an undignified scramble as the
self-imposed deadline of 20 November approached. The door had
been deliberately left open for a government 'man' to be included.
This in the end was Major John Glen, a former senior official at the
Ministry of Education. In the end also came Brum Henderson,
Managing Director of Ulster Television, who was helping to take
university education out of its maligned ivory tower and into the
popular marketplace of the small screen; he was seen also as a suitable
representative of the business community. Time ran so short that
Glen and Henderson had to be recruited by telephone and the
necessary paperwork done later. The committee was to be staffed by
serving officials W.T. Ewing and Zelda Davies, and supported by a
battery of advisers from various Northern Ireland government
ministries.

THE LOCKWOOD COMMITTEE IN ACTION

Despite the fact that the government intended to avoid re-doing
Robbins in an Ulster context and that it clearly expected the
Committee's report to be in at least draft form within a year, the
Committee's agenda was formidable including, as it did, the need to
make recommendations on teacher-training facilities as well as on
technological and agricultural education *and* the matter of a possible
new university. Every effort was to be made to conduct an inquiry
both broad and deep, but ideally in a fraction of the time required for
such an endeavour. The pressure was increased by the (apparently
unconsidered) reality that virtually all of the committee members had
full-time occupations and that half of them lived outside Ulster. An
unavoidable side-effect of this dilemma was that the Committee, and
Lockwood himself, was forced to depend heavily on the advisory
officials, many of whose opinions and data were conveyed through
W.T. Ewing. It should be emphasised that this in no way reflected any
sinister intent on the part of the government or its officials but rather
a certain reality of Ulster administrative etiquette with which
Lockwood would almost certainly have been unfamiliar. The fact was

that, unlike London where the post of Minister of the Crown was very much a full-time occupation, many members of successive Northern Ireland cabinets had continued to run their estates, farms, shirt factories and professional practices alongside their ministerial responsibilities, usually without any noticeable diminution in the quality of government. One almost inevitable effect of this way of doing things, however, was the placing of a greater degree of responsibility on the shoulders of the senior civil servants, who consequently had a greater degree of influence in government than was the case in Whitehall.

As Ewing and Davies struggled with timetables, travel arrangements and expense forms the Committee began a gruelling schedule of meetings (held alternately in Belfast and London), visits to Queen's University and Magee College, and the hearing of oral representations from hot-breathed local groups. The first of eighteen meetings was held in December 1963 and they continued at varying intervals until October 1964. The members had met on three occasions when, towards the end of January, representatives from the UGC paid a visit to advise the Committee on the question of establishing a new university. In an oblique reference to Queen's University the UGC officials pointed out that on the mainland it was the practice to consider the setting-up of a new university in situations where any bid to expand an existing college would be retarded by its location in a built-up area. It was felt that initially a 200-acre site would be the minimum suitable for a new and growing university. But alongside the *lebensraum* factor there were no-less important financial considerations. In terms of fresh construction work, priority would obviously have to be given to 'the provision of academic and other essential buildings' with purpose-built student residences following on subject to budgetary constraints.[6]

Idealised plans for new universities on the mainland with academic and amenity buildings on a central site and halls of residence 'on the periphery' had had to be abandoned as impracticable and over-expensive. University-planners therefore tended to seek 'a site within about two or three miles of the centre of the city with good transport communications and the usual services – water supplies, roads, electricity, drainage and so on – readily available'. On the point of student residences mainland planners had 'felt it necessary to consider

6 *University Development 1957–1962* (London, 1964), 99.

the supply of lodgings available in the area'. Such 'suitable lodgings, at reasonable prices, was [*sic*] therefore one of the factors, though not an overriding one' This was the received wisdom of the time with regard to new British universities and the UGC officials confirmed the same to the Lockwood Committee, adding only that such lodgings 'as a long-term solution ... were not desirable'.[7] The pattern would have been obvious to anyone who had monitored the establishment of recent new mainland universities or read the relevant parliamentary publications. They also took the opportunity to make it clear to the Committee, and doubtless to the Stormont officials also, that the UGC would furnish advice on a site *only* if the Northern Ireland government provided them with a range of possible locations *and* agreed to make the final decision in the matter independently of the UGC. Clearly the UGC was concerned to avoid a repeat performance of the frustrating consultation exercise of 1962.

The Committee had already visited Queen's and was soon to visit Magee. At Queen's it was evident that no solution was to be found to the problem of possible expansion. The city had grown to encompass the University; suitable sites were scarce, prices were prohibitively high. Magee, its small size notwithstanding, was in 1964 still on the edge of Londonderry but appreciably close to the city centre. The residential 'spread' had indeed caught up with the College but perhaps had not overtaken it to the point where suitable and affordable sites for expansion would have been impossible to find. But, as the Committee found, that was where tentative comparisons with Queen's had to end. The Londonderry City and County Borough had already submitted the city's case to be considered as the location for any new university. In the weeks before the Committee's visit to Magee a set of proposals on the same theme was received from the 'Coleraine University Promotion Committee', a body set up in March 1963 with repre-sentatives from four local councils and a chamber of commerce in the Coleraine area. These were: Portrush Urban District Council; Portstewart Urban District Council; Coleraine Rural District Council; Coleraine Borough Council; and Coleraine Chamber of Commerce. Also Lockwood had received a confidential letter from A.J. McConnell, Provost of Trinity College, Dublin, indicating that the future of the College's long-term relationship with Magee could no

7 See note 6 above.

7 Terence O'Neill (left) with Sir John Lockwood (copyright *Belfast Telegraph*).

longer be taken for granted. The Committee's tight schedule dictated that the visit to Magee had to be confined to a single day.

Founded in 1865 as a training college for Presbyterian clergymen, Magee had had a rollercoaster ride in terms of state recognition. The Royal University had extended recognition in 1881 but not to the point where Magee could acquire a charter and offer degrees. When in 1908 Queen's became a university and other Irish colleges were re-vamped as the National University of Ireland, Magee was again left out in the cold. Comfort was provided in some small measure the following year through the new arrangement with Trinity College, but as we have seen, by 1964 this connection was in danger. After the Second World War an attempt was made by the government to drag Magee, now severely under-developed and under-financed, into the twentieth century. The Acheson Committee, on which Terence O'Neill – Prime Minister in 1964 – had served, injected a capital gift

and an annual grant into the College's flaccid veins and tried to put
some distance between the sacred and the secular in its teaching
arrangements. A well-meaning (never very successful) attempt was
made to induce Queen's and Magee to enter into co-operation.
Ensuing legislation in 1953 established a Board of Trustees in an
(ultimately futile) effort to bring unity and order to the various
interested bodies associated with Magee.

The Lockwood Committee was confronted on its visit to Magee
with an administrative structure that was eccentric, unique (in
anyone's experience), and barely workable. The Trustees and their
concerns remained officially remote from the President and academic
staff. The Faculty Board was for professors only, effectively cutting
them off from the concerns of non-professorial staff. Staff had heard
that the Trinity connection was in jeopardy. Queen's had been nasty
to them – always. The Committee noted with dismay the atmosphere
of complacency; the seeming 'lack of dynamism', even in the senior
staff, which boded ill for any institution hoping to expand; the fact
that nobody appeared to have 'any clear ideas about how the College
should develop or what shape any future university development
in Londonderry should take'.[8] An important outcome of the visit was
that the Committee decided immediately to rule out Magee as a
nucleus of any future university development in Derry; nor was it
deemed worthy even of the status of a constituent college. The
'circumscribed mental outlook' and 'cramped physical situation'
noted by the Committee on its visit, together with the likelihood of
staffing problems and the need to somehow accommodate the
College's Presbyterian connection, were seen as a set of insurmount-
able difficulties.[9]

The city's claim to be the location of a new university, therefore,
was not helped by the written submission to the Committee by the
City and County Borough of Londonderry. The city's case was
overwhelmingly Magee-centred and concentrated on the College's
historical claims to preferment. The Committee studied the document
in vain for signs of the 'locations' criteria as conveyed by the UGC
officials and found instead the unimaginative proposal that future
students could be accommodated along current lines – by a mish-
mash of private lodgings and hostels. The submission of the Coleraine
Promotion Committee, on the other hand, referred directly to relevant

8 PRONI, ED 39/3.   9 See note 8.

publications dealing with those very criteria and had adapted their salient elements to inform and mould the argument in favour of Coleraine on a point-by-point basis. The example of Sussex and the concurrent plans for Essex were referred to. Also the local hoteliers representatives had been consulted and their 'enthusiasm and willingness' confirmed.[10]

When, therefore, the Committee at its eighth meeting in early May 1964 came to consider possible locations for a new university the members were acutely aware of a problem presented by the very existence of Magee: its historical claims as a college of third-level status (through its Trinity connection at least) would in almost any set of circumstances become a source of embarrassment and possibly undermine the credibility of a new university seeking to establish itself, no matter where in Ulster it was located. This precluded any immediate discussion of Londonderry as a possible location. Inevitably the Committee's attention turned to the Coleraine proposal, and by the end of the meeting the collective opinion of the members pointed 'inescapably' in one particular direction.[11]

In view of these developments the wearying task of hearing oral representations from local bodies, churches and professional associations was perhaps largely a public relations exercise. The claims of Armagh (never taken seriously at any time by the Committee) were dealt with rather cavalierly. The Coleraine representatives did not perform quite as well in person as they had on paper and, for obvious reasons, Lockwood avoided any expansiveness and worded his queries and comments with special care. Mindful of the Magee 'problem' he was no less careful in probing the views of the Londonderry Councillors seated before him regarding possible forms of a future relationship between Magee and the new university. The sensitivity of the situation was revealed when the Councillors bridled at a suggestion that the issue of the new university could be considered separately from Magee.

Despite the apparently obvious conclusion that was now indicated as regards the location of the new university, the committee-members were aware that in the absence of some resolution as to the future status of Magee their recommendation could not only embarrass the government politically but maybe risk compromising the establishment of the new institution. At the eleventh meeting, therefore, in

---

10 University of Ulster Archives, *A Second University for Northern Ireland: Proposals from the Coleraine/Portrush/Portstewart Area* [c1964]. 11 See note 8 above.

early June the Committee hammered out, with civil service advisers in attendance, the plus and minus factors regarding each possible location, except Magee which, it was firmly decided, 'should cease to function as a University College'.[12] As regards the basic matter of sites, adequate sites could be found in both Derry and Armagh, although some doubt had attached itself to the suitability of the two sites suggested near Coleraine. Significantly, however, the committee regarded both Derry and Armagh as places that were simply too poor and underdeveloped to support a growing university. Having reached this conclusion, the Committee hesitated even though the list of points in favour of Coleraine far exceeded those against the area. The officials, sensing a possible impasse, intervened with a piece of fresh information from the UGC: no money would be provided in the immediate future for halls of residence, only for academic buildings. Also, a long-neglected fact, it was common practice for the UGC to check the availability of potential student accommodation in areas for which arguments had been advanced in favour of location. To depart from UGC policy in such a matter, the officials warned, would oblige the Committee to produce strong justifications. In a sense, by tipping the balance in this manner, the officials had silently agreed to take from the Committee's shoulders onto their own the immediate responsibility for the political fall-out which Lockwood feared might accompany a decision in favour of Coleraine. However, it was Lockwood and not the officials who would have to sign the published report.

THE NORTHERN IRELAND GOVERNMENT AND THE
LOCKWOOD REPORT

Terence O'Neill presided over a Cabinet divided uneasily between hawks and doves. O'Neill himself was committed to improving relations with the government of the Irish Republic and to convincing disgruntled northern Nationalists that the state could work for them as well as it did for Unionists. The hawks, mindful of the recent IRA campaign, the rising expectations of a better-educated and more vocal Catholic community, and the fact that the Republic's constitution still brazenly asserted jurisdiction over Northern Irish territory, felt that O'Neill's gestures were mistimed and ill-advised. Against this back-

12 See note 8 above.

GOVERNMENT OF NORTHERN IRELAND

HIGHER EDUCATION
in Northern Ireland

Report of the Committee appointed by
the Minister of Finance

Presented to Parliament by Command of
His Excellency the Governor of Northern Ireland
February 1965

BELFAST
HER MAJESTY'S STATIONERY OFFICE
Reprinted 1965
PRICE £1 0s. 0d. NET

Cmd. 475

8 The Lockwood Report: title page.

drop the imminence of a new university should have been the Good News for 1965. It wasn't. When the ministers came to consider Lockwood's draft report on December 1964 and again in January, there was dismay at the proposal that Magee should cease to be a University College. After much wrangling it was decided to issue a White Paper in which the relevant paragraph was re-worded to reflect the government's disagreement with the recommendation. 'Accordingly', the amended paragraph went on, 'the government proposes to investigate further whether the College can be incorporated in the new university ...'. The White Paper, entitled *Higher Education in Northern Ireland: Government Statement on the Report of the Committee appointed by the Minister of Finance*, was published on the same day as Lockwood's Report. In most other respects, including the siting of the new university at Coleraine, the Report was deemed acceptable. On reflection, later in 1965, the government was to reject the Lockwood recommendation that agricultural studies should be transferred from Queen's to the new university. Important for the structure of the future University of Ulster was Lockwood's recommendation that the Regional College of Technology was to join forces with the Colleges of Art and Domestic Science to form an 'Ulster College': this institution was to be the forerunner of the Ulster Polytechnic.

FALL-OUT

By the time the Lockwood Report, officially entitled *Higher Education in Northern Ireland: Report of the Committee appointed by the Minister of Finance*, was published in February 1965 the location secret had leaked out and a 'University for Derry Committee', involving Unionists as well as Nationalists, had been formed in the hope of overturning the recommendation. Nor did the political fall-out end there. It had long been an article of faith amongst Nationalists that successive Unionist governments had on political and sectarian grounds deliberately starved the north-western areas of Northern Ireland of resources and capital and had tried to downgrade and impoverish the area socially and economically. This 'conspiracy theory' was based on a mixture of verifiable realities, misperceptions and suspicion. It reflected deep disenchantment with employment opportunities, housing and voting rights, as well as with the failure to maintain decent road and rail communications and a myriad of other grievances. Now, it seemed, the government and its Committee were going to deny Derry the golden chance for socio-economic regeneration which, it was believed, would have accompanied the location of the new university in the city.

Public manifestations of displeasure with Lockwood's report included the holding of the largest protest meeting ever seen in the city and the spectacle of a motorcade from Derry to Stormont involving some 2,000 cars. The report was also the subject of the longest and most bitter parliamentary debate in the state's history. Lockwood and his English colleagues had been aware that certain sectarian and political tensions did exist in Ulster; but, like most mainlanders in the early 1960s, they had no idea of the depth and

9 Magee students lead 1965 protests against Lockwood's recommendation that the
new university be sited at Coleraine (copyright Willie Carson Collection).

intensity of these sentiments. At the end of the 1950s an Ulster commercial firm, having conducted a survey on the 'average' Englishman's knowledge of Northern Ireland, made the depressing discovery that around half the respondents 'did not know what Ulster was,' or that it had its own government; or had taken part in the Second World War; and that many believed it was part of the Irish Republic, or Scotland, or even 'an independent state'.[13]

AFTERMATH

In the days and weeks following the emergence of the Report the government, mainly through its attorney-general who was MP for Londonderry, made various attempts at damage-limitation, but all to no avail. The outcry continued, the hawks gathered threateningly, and O'Neill secured parliamentary acceptance of the Report by a mere eight votes (27 to 19). The government kept its promise as expressed in the amended paragraph of the Report 'to investigate further' the possible incorporation of Magee in the new university. But all discussions of tentative solutions and proposals with Magee representatives and with the UGC dissolved into inconclusiveness before the seeming probability that no Academic Planning Board would accept the extraordinary situation: the government had rejected the clear recommendation of its own Committee of experts and had passed an essentially *political* problem onto a body of academics tasked with setting up the new university. In a worst-case scenario, it was even possible that no such Board would even be formed and the whole prospect of a new university put in jeopardy. In the short term no satisfactory solution to the Magee 'problem' could be found. At its first meeting in October 1965 the Academic Planning Board was reminded by its secretary, the same W.T. Ewing who had served the Lockwood Committee, of the government's crucial amendment to Lockwood's Report and that this had been incorporated into the Board's terms of reference. The Board, clearly dismayed, resolved that it would not allow the Magee 'problem' to sidetrack if from its principal duty of establishing the new university. The troubled history of the New University of Ulster had begun.

13 James Loughlin, *Ulster Unionism and British National Identity since 1885* (London & New York, 1995), 173.

3

The New University of Ulster

ARTHUR P. WILLIAMSON

'Chill winds, changes and erosions have had to be endured in the growth of this University.' [1]

The New University of Ulster was founded at Coleraine in 1966 and received its Royal Charter in 1970. Its first students arrived in late September 1968 and moved into flats and guesthouses in nearby Portstewart and Portrush. The University incorporated Magee College in Londonderry, established in 1865 as a Presbyterian liberal arts and theological foundation. Having had sixteen intakes of students, it was merged in 1984 with the Ulster Polytechnic to form the University of Ulster. The New University had awarded some 5,000 first degrees, 600 Master's degrees, 650 diplomas and 1,000 certificates and other awards. More than forty years on, in 2006/7 over 9,000 undergraduates and postgraduates were studying at Coleraine and Magee, 5,597 and 3,538 respectively.

The Robbins Report, published in October 1963, reflected and promoted an unprecedented increase in the number of British universities. New universities had opened, or were being planned, at Sussex, Bath, York, East Anglia, Lancaster, Essex, Warwick, Kent and Stirling. In Northern Ireland a growing body of opinion was pressing the Unionist government to widen access to advanced further and higher education and to establish a second university. Universities throughout the United Kingdom, including Queen's, were experiencing severe pressure from new applicants and in November 1963 the Northern Ireland government announced the establishment of a committee on higher education to be chaired by Sir John Lockwood. Lockwood was a highly experienced choice for he had extensive knowledge of university planning. He had recently worked in Africa

---

1 Professor Frank Lelièvre presenting the retired first Vice-Chancellor, Professor Alan Burges, for the degree of Doctor of Science in 1977.

with senior higher education planners from the United States. Lockwood's concept of a second university in Northern Ireland was much influenced by the model of the land-grant colleges in the United States, many of which became state universities. They had made major contributions to the social and economic development of their regions and catered for a broad spectrum of students. Combining British and American ideas, Lockwood's vision was of an 'umbrella' institution which would remove the artificial barrier between higher and further education.[2] This vision was not realised until two decades later when the United Kingdom's first umbrella university of the kind he had envisaged resulted from the merger of the New University of Ulster and the Ulster Polytechnic. Lockwood did not live to see the results of his work in Northern Ireland for he died in 1965, shortly after his report was published.

Lockwood's Report indicated that the Committee 'regard the provision of a second university in Northern Ireland as a matter of the greatest urgency'.[3] They recommended that the University should be established at Coleraine; that it should be innovative, facilitating experimentation in unusual subjects and combinations of subjects; and that it should emphasise interdisciplinarity. By 1980 it was expected to have an enrolment of between 5,000 and 6,000 full-time students studying the biological and related pure and applied sciences, the environmental and social sciences, the humanities and teacher education. A Faculty of Agriculture should be established as a foundational part of the university and the existing arrangements between Queen's University and the Ministry of Agriculture, under which the Ministry employed the staff in the Faculty of Agriculture at Queen's, should be terminated.

SHAPING THE UNIVERSITY

In May 1965 members of the University Grants Committee visited Coleraine and spent two hours looking at four sites in different parts of the locality. An official stood by with gumboots in case of bad weather but the Committee worked in ideal early summer conditions.

2 Lockwood's vision of an 'umbrella' university is set out in his *Report on the Development of a University in Northern Rhodesia*, Lusaka, 1964.   3 *Higher Education in Northern Ireland: Report of a Committee appointed by the Ministry of Finance*, [Chaired by Sir John Lockwood], para. 184.

10 NUU's Academic Planning Board in session.

A decision was taken in favour of some 300 acres at Ballysally on the northern outskirts of Coleraine, consisting of poorly drained and fairly flat farmland, used for pasture and arable crops. The bleak location was ameliorated by the site's aspect to the River Bann and its views of the beautiful North Coast and Donegal hills. Nine months later the local authorities vested the land and presented it to the embryo university. Regrettably, local farmers were deprived of their farms before compensation agreements had been concluded. They and their neighbours formed a blockade of tractors to oppose the entry of the contractors – an inauspicious beginning to relations with the local community.

Assisted by the University Grants Committee, the Department of Education assembled an Academic Planning Board, with Sir James Cook, a distinguished organic chemist, as Chairman. He was Vice-Chancellor of Exeter University and had served on the Academic Planning Board at Warwick. Like Lockwood, he had considerable experience of higher education planning and development in Africa. The other members included two prominent academics from the University of London, Professor G.C. Allen, a political scientist, and Professor C.T. Ingold, a botanist; Professor W.H.G. Armytage of Sheffield University who had written widely on models of higher education in various countries; Professor D.C. Harrison, a distinguished scientist recently retired from Queen's University; Mrs E.M. Chilver, Principal of Lady Margaret Hall, Oxford; Dr A.G. Lehmann, Director of the Linguaphone Institute; and Dr J.S. Hawnt, formerly

Director of Education for Belfast. Its secretary was Mr W.T. Ewing, a civil servant in the Department of Education who had served the Lockwood Committee in a similar capacity. The Board held a total of sixteen meetings until July 1970 when the University, having obtained its Royal Charter, became autonomous. By the time of the Board's first meeting in October 1965 the government had rejected two of Lockwood's key recommendations: that Magee College should be closed and that the Faculty of Agriculture at Queen's should become the foundation faculty of the new university. Government had decreed that Agriculture remain at Queen's and that Magee be incorporated into the new institution. These early decisions had far-reaching implications for the development of the University.

At early meetings pressing matters were the selection of a Vice-Chancellor and a Registrar, decisions on the academic structure and initial range of subjects, the identification of planning consultants and, notably, arrangements for assimilating Magee College. Of cardinal importance was the drafting of the Charter which had to wait for the first round of appointments and until some of the first Professors were in post, to allow the Interim Senate to contribute to its drafting. Relations with Queen's University were a concern. Self-protective instincts at Queen's were soon felt in relation to the selection of a name for the University. That chosen by the Academic Planning Board, with strong local support, was 'The University of Ulster'. This was opposed by Queen's. The compromise eventually agreed, very reluctantly by the Interim Council, was to insert the adjective 'New'.

On 22 February 1966 the Minister of Education, W.K. Fitzsimmons, announced that the Academic Planning Board had appointed as Vice-Chancellor, Dr Alan Burges, an Australian, Professor of Botany and Senior Pro-Vice Chancellor at Liverpool University; and a recent past President of both the British Ecological Society and the British Mycological Society. An early priority for him was the appointment of the University's first senior academics and administrators, which was accomplished by autumn 1967. The first meeting of the Interim Senate on 5 October 1967 comprised the Vice-Chancellor, six existing Professors from Magee and seven newly appointed Professors at Coleraine. Those from Magee were Clark (French), Guthrie (Mathematics), Lelièvre (Greek and Latin), McCracken (History), Nicholl (Philosophy), and Warner (English). The newly-appointed Professors at Coleraine were Gibson (Economics), Murphy (Russian), Wallace (History), Oldfield (Geography), Sheddick (Social

11 The University Sponsoring Committee, Coleraine, 1966.

Organisation), Newbould (Biology), Tredgold (Physics). Amyan Macfadyen, who had just taken up his appointment as Professor of Biology, was not present at this meeting.

The initiative to promote the establishment of a university at Coleraine was taken by Mr John W. Moore, a prominent Coleraine businessman who assembled a sponsoring committee comprising thirty-four members drawn from the Coleraine Chamber of Commerce, Coleraine Urban District Council and adjacent local authorities. It established a limited company: 'The Executive Council for the Establishment of a University in the Coleraine Area'. With nine members including the new Vice-Chancellor, its chairman was John W. Moore, who was succeeded by Mr Ronald McCulloch, Managing Director of Monsanto's Acrilan plant in Coleraine. At a meeting in July 1966 of 'The University Company', as it was known, the Chairman reported that Mr W.T. Ewing had been appointed University Registrar by the Academic Planning Board. He also became the Chairman of the Trustees of the Garfield Weston Bequest

12 John W. Moore (*centre*) and colleagues inspecting the
Coleraine site and plan, mid-1960s.

of £250,000 to the University's Foundation Appeal. From then until
the merger in 1984 Mr Ewing's office provided the secretariat for the
Council and its Finance Committee, and for the Senate, giving him
huge influence over the governance of the University. On the granting
of the University's Royal Charter the Executive Council meta-
morphosed into the Council of the New University of Ulster, the
body responsible for governance, for the employment of staff and for
the discharge of legal and financial responsibilities.

PHYSICAL DEVELOPMENT

By April 1966 the die was cast for the physical development of the
university site at Coleraine. The Academic Planning Board appointed
Sir Robert Matthew, Johnston-Marshall and partners to prepare a
plan. Simultaneously the Ministry of Development commissioned an

associated firm of consultants, Percy Johnston-Marshall and Associates, to prepare a development plan for the Coleraine, Portstewart, Portrush 'Triangle' area, and for the physical (including landscape) development of the university site. The Matthew Johnston-Marshall partnership had provided the development plans for the new universities at York, Bath and Stirling.

The consultants' final *Report on the Development Plan* (1968) set out the anticipated physical shape of the University: a two-stage building programme, the first for 3,500 students and the second to provide for a total of 6,000, the first target to be reached by 1973 and the second by 1980. The first permanent building, known as Phase One (later South Buildings), consisted of 146,000 square feet. Construction commenced in May 1967 and fourteen months later the university began commissioning the other buildings. The main building, known as Phase Two (later Central Buildings), was a three-storey Spine with the Library occupying the entire top floor. Accommodation for the Schools of the University, apart from the Education Centre which had a separate building and library, was attached to different points of the Spine. At the front of the site a nine-storey Tower Block, visible from Coleraine, contained a suite of offices for the Vice-Chancellor and Registrar as well as administrative accommodation and some teaching space. A feature of the University buildings was the 'Diamond', an auditorium providing accommodation for examinations, for graduations and for large conferences and seating some 1,500 people, which was completed in 1974. The Diamond provides a regional centre for concerts by the Ulster Orchestra and has led to the Coleraine campus becoming a centre for cultural activities in the north of Northern Ireland. Building work on Phase Two commenced in the autumn of 1969. The School of Biological and Environmental Studies moved into its new accommodation in the autumn of 1970 and the other sections were occupied in 1971, 1972 and 1973 respectively. 'Phase Two', the main complex of the University, was linked to the Phase One buildings by a covered way facilitating the integration of students and staff at the Education Centre (located in Phase One) with the rest of the University.

Professor Mike Shattock, renowned first Registrar at Warwick University, once suggested that 'a beautiful campus is a jewel in the crown of any university'.[4] At Coleraine, significantly, the development

4 Speaking at the University of Ulster's Senior Staff Conference at the Hilton Hotel, Templepatrick, 17 May 2001.

13 The Coleraine campus overlooking the River Bann.

of the campus landscape, alongside buildings and other facilities, was planned from the University's inception. Chiefly responsible for the outcome was Dr David Willis, Grounds Superintendent 1973–84, who was strongly supported by Professor Palmer Newbould and other staff and students. Donations of trees, shrubs and plants came from many quarters including the Baronscourt estate of the Chancellor, the Duke of Abercorn. A virtually treeless landscape required the planting of massive shelterbelts behind which less robust species might thrive. Further developments included the Guy L. Wilson Daffodil Garden, formally launched in 1974 by Professor Fergus Wilson, nephew of the celebrated Northern Ireland daffodil breeder, Guy Wilson, and the Augustine Henry Garden, laid out in 1982 to mark the centenary of that famous collector's first foray into China. In 1979 the University hosted the World Daffodil Convention. The Daffodil Garden achieved heritage status in 1981 and a year later

14 The Guy L. Wilson Daffodil Garden at Coleraine.

became the National Narcissus Collection. The campus at Coleraine is now one of the most attractive parklands in Northern Ireland.

ACADEMIC FOUNDATIONS AND FOCUS

Lockwood insisted that 'the development of the new institution should be with a practical objective'. Echoing his experience in Africa, and his work with leading American higher education planners, he believed that 'there is no fundamental reason why universities should not have practical as well as academic objectives in view'.[5] The educational spectrum proposed for the University included the Biological and related Pure and Applied Sciences; the Environmental and Human Sciences; the Social Sciences and Teacher Education. There was a strong steer in favour of interdisciplinary studies and academic structures to facilitate them. The School of Studies concept, invented at Sussex, and developed at East Anglia, was adopted. This model envisaged a base of academic activity from a wide field and provided a flexible academic organisation which (as later at the Ulster

5 Lockwood Report, paras. 135, 192.

Polytechnic) encouraged interdisciplinary study and discouraged excessive specialisation.

Reflecting recent thinking at London University, the basic teaching unit was standardized and, in most first-degree courses, eighteen units were studied over three years. In addition, substantially anticipating national changes some twenty years later, the University adopted a system under which each academic year was divided into two semesters. Along with formal examinations, cumulative assessment, which had been pioneered at East Anglia, was common to all degree programmes. Interdisciplinarity was fostered in that each course provided opportunities for the study of up to three optional units chosen from outside the student's main academic area. Moreover, 'combined programmes' catered for study of both a major and a minor field, while there were several 'integrated' programmes which drew on units from various subject areas. All these elements of flexibility also allowed students to delay their final choice of degree programme until the start of their second year of study. Among the first Professors these arrangements were contentious, some arguing that unless students successfully completed particular units at certain stages in three-year programmes, their education would be deficient. Most, however, were firmly committed to the values of interdisciplinarity and delayed choice.

Echoing Lockwood, the Academic Planning Board decided that, during its first five to ten years, the University would consist of five academic divisions, namely four Schools and an Education Centre. The Schools were Biological and Environmental Studies; Physical Sciences; Social Sciences; and Humanities. Twenty 'subjects' were divided between the four Schools and the Education Centre, the latter providing for the professional teaching of education and for subjects such as Art and Physical Education, not taught elsewhere in the University.

The government had accepted the principle of Lockwood's recommendations about teacher training, including the concept of an Education Centre. Each of the four Schools taught students of Education alongside other students registered in those schools. The flexibility of the unit structure made such an arrangement possible and facilitated the academic and social integration of students of Education. Students enrolled in the Education Centre followed degree programmes in other Schools and simultaneously undertook 'concurrent' studies in teacher education, together with periods of teaching practice, throughout their four years in what comprised one of the most successful innovations of the New University. The Education Centre also offered a non-graduate

Certificate in Education, with less demanding entrance requirements than degree programmes. Many students were able to transfer at the end of their first year of the Certificate onto a three-year, or a four-year, single subject programme or combined programme, inclusive of a teaching qualification. The establishment of the Education Centre stimulated developments at Queen's for, coinciding with the first intake of students at Coleraine, Queen's established both a Faculty of Education and an Institute of Education with a widely representative governing body, headed by a Director.

The Librarian, Mr F.J.E. Hurst, formerly librarian at Trinity College, Dublin, was appointed in April 1967. He and his staff began to accumulate books in a converted Dutch hay barn in a corner of the Coleraine site. Later they moved to purpose-built accommodation in the Phase One building where there were spaces for 340 readers; and later still into the main Library, taking up the entire top floor of Phase II. From its beginnings the Library employed automated equipment to assist with processing its holdings. Automation was rapidly developed and by 1977 the Library was described as 'the most comprehensive exponent of library automation in Ireland'.[6] Over the years the Library received major collections from philanthropic donors, perhaps the most significant of which were 5,000 items which had belonged to Sir James Headlam-Morley, a senior British delegate at the Peace of Versailles, and the Henry Davis Collection. The latter, (valued at more than £5 million) comprises some 200 books including sixty incunabula, a leaf from the Gutenberg Bible, the first book printed using moveable type, a vellum copy of a Bible printed in Mainz by Fust and Schoeffer (1462), and a first edition of Milton's *Areopagitica* (1644). The Magee library had a number of special collections and among its rare books are 700 volumes printed before 1700 and siege pamphlets from 1689.

THE RIVERSIDE THEATRE

A notable feature of the University, and one supported by the Arts Council for Northern Ireland and by Coleraine Borough Council, was the Riverside Theatre. Designed by Peter Moro, a disciple of Le

6 B.J.C. Wintour and B. McDowell, 'Automation at the New University of Ulster', *Program*, vol. 10 (2), April 1976, 60–74.

15 The Riverside Theatre, Coleraine.

Corbusier, this ambitious project was initiated and managed by a committee led by Mrs Evelyn Burges, indefatigable wife of the Vice-Chancellor. Built with funding from the University's Foundation Appeal and from the Gulbenkian Foundation, its striking features were an imaginative addition to the University buildings. The Queen opened the theatre in August 1977 during her Jubilee visit to the University. Later that year the Riverside received the prestigious Architect's ward for one of the United Kingdom's best public design features of 1977. The Theatre Club was notably successful in engaging volunteers from the local community. As well as welcoming visiting companies, the Riverside provided a superb venue for local operatic and drama societies and was the venue for the finals of the national one-act drama competition. The theatre provided a training ground for many young actors, of whom the best known is James Nesbitt. An early member of the Riverside's Youth Theatre, he was discovered in 1978 while playing the part of the Artful Dodger in Lionel Bart's *Oliver* in that year's Christmas Show.

THE INCORPORATION OF MAGEE

How to incorporate Magee College into the New University was a
challenge to the Academic Planning Board and the Vice-Chancellor,
and a matter of considerable anxiety in Derry. In May 1965 the
Minister of Education announced the details of an agreement
concluded with the Trustees of the College. Magee would be a
constituent College of the University, represented on its governing
body and offering undergraduate courses, including honours, in a
range of subjects in Arts, including Economics and Geography. The
University assumed direct responsibility for maintaining academic
activities at or above their current level. This ended the arrangement
between the College and Trinity College Dublin, under which since
1908 students at Magee had completed their studies at Trinity and
graduated with University of Dublin degrees.

The future of Magee continued to be controversial. Student
numbers were in decline: in autumn 1971 new enrolments totalled
only sixty-three, and the entire student body was a mere 180, a
reduction on the previous year. Although unanticipated, this was
scarcely surprising given that, by the early 1970s, some of the worst
civil disorder in living memory was occurring frequently within a few
hundred yards of the campus. On 11 January 1972 the Senate voted
by twenty-seven votes to six that 'there is no viable future for
undergraduate studies at Magee University College and recommends
to Council that undergraduate studies there be transferred to the
Coleraine site of the University'.[7] In place of undergraduate studies,
it was decided to establish an Institute of Continuing Education at
Magee, of which more later.

STUDENT NUMBERS AND RECRUITMENT

If inadequate numbers were a problem at Magee, they were also an
early and persistent concern at Coleraine. In 1972 anxieties were
voiced in the *Times Higher Education Supplement*. Instead of having
2,200 students, the University had some 1,600. In March 1974
Brigadier Ronald Broadhurst, Unionist Assemblyman for South Down,
initiated a critical exchange at Stormont on the New University,

7 University of Ulster Archives, NUU Senate minutes, 11 January 1972.

claiming that its resources might be better spent on building up Queen's to become a 'University of distinction'.[8] Within the University Broadhurst's remarks touched a raw nerve. The Senate discussed the disappointing numbers of applications and it was suggested that some of the University's selectors were turning away suitable applicants. Then in May Peter McLachlan, Assemblyman for South Antrim, asked: 'Could it be that we only need one university, sited perhaps in more than one place, but run conjointly?'[9]

The following table indicates the respective shares of the Northern Ireland undergraduate population registered at Queen's University, the New University and the Ulster Polytechnic during the 1970s. While student numbers remained very similar at Queen's and increased slightly at NUU, they grew from 12.8 per cent to 40 per cent of the total at the Ulster College/Polytechnic.

Several observations are relevant. Firstly, Lockwood could not have envisaged that degree-level study, validated by the Council for National Academic Awards (CNAA), would take place at the Ulster College. CNAA was established in 1965, only a few months after Lockwood had finished his work. Its subject panels approved the award of academic degrees at polytechnics and other non-university institutions. Secondly, his report recommended that Government establish effective coordinating machinery to oversee the provision of undergraduate places in Northern Ireland, but the government's leadership in this matter was weak and this did not take place. Thirdly, and most significantly, Lockwood and others assumed for forecasting purposes that the numbers entering Northern Ireland from elsewhere in the UK would roughly balance the outflow of students. During the 'Troubles' the annual haemorrhage of students from Northern Ireland was about equal to those of a small university, whereas the inflow was negligible. In 1971–2 the proportion of Northern Ireland students who were undergraduates in Great Britain was 25 per cent. One year later it was 32 per cent, and by 1973–4 the percentage had risen to 40. Given the emergence of entirely new patterns of student migration following the onset of the 'Troubles', there was no possibility of NUU meeting the UGC's target of 3,465 students by 1977–8.

8 'Brigadier Broadhurst Wants University Scrapped,' *Belfast Telegraph*, 7 March 1974.
9 Northern Ireland Assembly *Proceedings*, 8 May 1974, col. 760.

Changes in institutional shares of student numbers, 1971/72 and 1978/79.[10]

Institution	1971/72		1979/80	
	FTE	*% of all students remaining in N. Ireland for study*	*FTE*	*% of all students remaining in N. Ireland for study*
Queen's University	5,492	68.9	5,453	46.7
New University	1,474	18.5	1,551	13.3
Ulster College	1,024	12.8	4,672	40.0
Totals	7,972		11,676	

Note: Due to rounding percentages may not total 100.

CULTURAL ACTIVITIES

A considerable number of the academic staff and some administrators originated from outside Northern Ireland. Staff and students together were a cosmopolitan and culturally diverse addition to the community life of the 'Triangle' area. The early years saw flourishing cultural activities. Walter Allen, the first Professor of English, appointed certain staff specifically because of their commitment to the practice of drama, music and poetry as part of teaching programmes. Students were encouraged to participate in live productions of plays they studied. An active Drama Society attracted students and staff from many departments. Early productions included Jean Anouilh's *Antigone* (in Portrush Town Hall) and *Romeo and Juliet* (in Coleraine Town Hall). Music was also strong and there were frequent lunchtime recitals by talented staff and students. In 1971 'The Culture Circus', a group of over 50 staff and students, toured to Berlin and Frankfurt with a repertoire that included a jazz ensemble and several original student plays. The Film Society had a huge membership and each

10 Re-analysis of Table 8.1, Statistical Supplement to the Chilver Report, *The Future of Higher Education in Northern Ireland,* 1982.

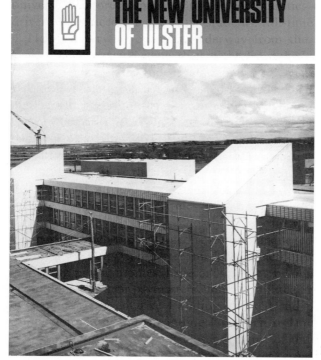

THE NEW UNIVERSITY OF ULSTER

16 NUU's first prospectus.

week during term it screened three programmes. Student newspapers came and went. They included *Phase One, Satyr, Scribe, Epsilon, Phase Three*, and *The Triangle Free Press*. One memorable paper, the satirical *Ballysally Gazette*, provided a topical, amusing but fair commentary on all aspects of life at the University. In the University's early days Ulster Television provided the equipment for a television studio that was widely used by staff and students. Later, after the establishment of Communication Studies in 1978, the same company provided an annual prize for the best student in that field.

THE CHAPLAINCY

The Academic Planning Board firmly intended, and openly declared, that the University would be a secular institution, a stance that led to considerable public concern and resistance. It was later agreed that there would be four chaplains, representing the four main churches, nominated by their church and appointed, but not salaried, by the

Council. On the initiative of Revd Ian Paisley at the University Court, it was subsequently acknowledged that the Council had the power to appoint chaplains from other denominations, but this was not exercised. Quite apart from the energetic contributions of individual chaplains, one hugely positive outcome emerged from all this. Throughout the University's existence successive Roman Catholic chaplains were jointly responsible with a Lecturer in Education (who was also an ordained member of the Church of Ireland) for the teaching of religious education in the Education Centre. This was a rare, valued and much applauded example of an integrated approach to an area fraught with difficulty in Northern Ireland.

SPORT AND RECREATION

Shortly after the first students arrived the Athletic Union was established to coordinate sport and recreation for staff and students. The Union was modelled on the Athletic Union at Manchester University. Its Finance Committee allocated funds to the university's sports clubs and the President's Plate was annually presented to an outstanding athlete. Staff lobbied effectively for funds to provide facilities for sport and recreation and the University developed a very good range of playing fields which were well used. Many students remained in Coleraine at weekends and staff and student members of the Union established some 30 sports clubs. Among outdoor sports rugby and soccer predominated at first. In the mid-1970s the Soccer Club won the All-Ireland Universities' League, a notable achievement for Ireland's newest university. The University also had thriving cricket, gaelic and hockey clubs. The NUU team won the opening Irish Universities' Cricket Association tournament, beating both Queen's and Trinity. The Rowing Club used the splendid and convenient facilities of the River Bann. Successful indoor sports activities included judo and fencing. A high point came in 1980 when, notwithstanding the 'Troubles', the Athletic Union hosted the World University Cross Country Championship, which was televised on *Sportsview*. Salient features of sport at the University were its cross-community ethos and well-above-average levels of participation by staff and students in sporting and recreational activities.

TEACHING AND RESEARCH

By 1972–3 the University offered a total of fifty-nine undergraduate
degree programmes of which eleven were joint programmes between
Schools and the Education Centre. The University subsequently
developed new academic subjects, including Psychology, Nursing
Studies, Accounting, Communication Studies, Banking and Finance,
Medical Laboratory Science and Computing Science. Academic
development, therefore, was progressive and cumulative.

Biological and Environmental Studies had been identified by
Lockwood as a foundational field of study. The two Professors of
Biology were Amyan Macfadyen, who became President of the British
Ecological Society from 1970 to 1972 and Palmer Newbould, who was
greatly involved in environmental education and contributed at the
European level to OECD and the Council of Europe. They were soon
joined by Dr Brian Wood who became Director of the Limnology
Laboratory at Traad Point on Lough Neagh, and by Professor Frank
Oldfield, a geographer and palaeo-ecologist. The Biology honours
degree offered either a broad range of biological subjects especially
suitable for students wishing to study Biology together with the
concurrent Education degree, or special final-year options for students
wishing to undertake research in, for example, microbiology or
limnology. Psychology was established in 1973 and initially was
headed by Professor Richard Lynn.

The School of Physical Sciences comprised four subject areas:
Chemistry, Physics, Mathematics and Computing Science (established
in the late 1970s). Chemistry was headed by Professors Michael
Grundon and Findlay Swinton, joined as Professor in the early 1980s
by Bill Watts, when eleven members of staff were responsible for an
honours degree programme in single subject Chemistry and
contributed to degrees in Biological Chemistry and in Chemistry with
Education. During the later 1970s more than half the annual output
of honours Chemistry graduates in Northern Ireland were being
educated at the New University. The course in Biological Chemistry
was very popular and produced a substantial proportion of Northern
Ireland's honours graduates in biochemistry. Chemistry research at
Coleraine had a head start with the move of nine research personnel
accompanying members of staff from Queen's University, Belfast and
from the University of Glasgow. An early encouragement, in 1972,

was the results of a survey in which Chemistry at the University of Ulster was designated nationally as a 'centre of excellence'.

The first Professor of Physics was R.H. Tredgold. Dr Gareth Roberts was appointed Senior Lecturer in Physics in 1968, was rapidly promoted to a Chair and became Head of School and Dean of the Faculty of Science. In 1984, after leaving the University, he was appointed FRS, and later became a very influential chairman of the Committee of Vice-Chancellors and Principals and Master of Wolfson College, Oxford. Dr Robin H. Williams was appointed to a personal Chair in Physics for his work on surface science. He subsequently became Vice-Chancellor of the University of Swansea and an FRS. Academic staff in Physics offered an honours degree in Physics and contributed to degree programmes in Applied Physics and Environmental Physics. Professor Andrew Young, earlier a colleague of the Vice-Chancellor at Liverpool University, established Mathematics, with a particular emphasis on Applied Mathematics. Professor Ralph Henstock, internationally known for his work on integrals, joined the School later.

The School of Social Sciences included Economics, Social Administration (plus Applied Social Studies), Sociology and Anthropology and, after 1975, Nursing Studies. The initial Professors were Norman Gibson (an economist who was the School's first Dean) and Vernon Sheddick, Professor of Social Organisation. John Spencer was appointed as a second Professor of Economics, specialising in Econometrics. In 1971 a degree in Economics with Accounting was established. Economics, Human Geography and Planning were taught jointly with staff from Geography. Training for social workers commenced in 1969 with the inauguration of a postgraduate course in Applied Social Studies. The popularity of the subject among both undergraduates and postgraduates was such that Social Administration became one of the largest subjects in the University. From the earliest days the School pursued a vigorous programme of research on contemporary social policy issues in Northern Ireland. The School provided a base for the interdisciplinary Centre for the Study of Conflict which, together with the Ethnic Studies Network, became an internationally known focus for the study of conflict and conflict resolution.

Until 1972 the School of Humanities was located both at Coleraine (where it was led by Professor Paul Christophersen) and at Magee College (by Professor Alan Warner). Subsequently, after the amalgamation of the Sub-Schools which followed the termination of undergraduate studies at Magee in 1972, Terence O'Keefe, a philosopher, was elected to the deanship of the School of Humanities. At Coleraine staff in English offered a single subject degree and a number of combinations, of which the most popular was English with Education. From the beginning the emphasis in History was on modern and contemporary history and a History Film and Sound Archive was established to support teaching. The subject attracted large student numbers from its early days. A part-time Diploma/Master's degree in twentieth century history was popular with teachers and attracted students from across Northern Ireland and beyond.

In 1974, two years after all undergraduate teaching had been centralised on the Coleraine campus, the teaching of modern languages was brought together under the Board of Modern Languages and European Studies with, as the respective Professorial heads: Brian Murphy (Russian); John Renwick and later Robert McBride (French); Frank Jolles (German); and later Seamus MacMathuna (Irish). The Board offered eight collaborative undergraduate degrees combining the opportunity to study language and literature in many combinations. Prior to 1972 Philosophy, together with English and History, was taught at undergraduate level at both Coleraine and at Magee. Philosophy was led by Professor Harry Nicholl and, following the transfer to Coleraine, staff in Philosophy developed a range of imaginative programmes, with an emphasis on applied ethics and leading to degrees in Philosophy and, in combination, not just Philosophy with other Humanities disciplines, but also with Sociology and Psychology.

The Education Centre quickly became one of the United Kingdom's largest university departments of education and initially teacher training was the only professional field, apart from social work, which the University Grants Committee permitted the University to establish. (Later Accountancy, Nursing Studies and Medical Laboratory Sciences were developed very successfully.) Professor Alan Milton and Professor Jim Hendry established the Education Centre. The former had been Acting Principal of the University College of Rhodesia and had wide experience as a professor of education and former teacher. He believed firmly in the principle of concurrent teacher education, whereby teachers were trained while they pursued studies in their main academic field. Professor Malcolm Skilbeck was Director of the Education Centre from 1972 to 1975 and developed for serving teachers the immensely popular Diploma in Advanced Studies in

Education. Other professorial staff in Education were Hugh Sockett (who subsequently moved to Magee to become Director of the Institute of Continuing Education), Joe Nesbitt, David Jenkins and Alan Rogers, a very strong and experienced team.

The University's potential in the field of research was evident from the beginning. In its first two years there were 246 academic publications with 64 each from the Schools of Physical Sciences and of Biological and Environmental Studies, 58 from Humanities and 5 from the Vice-Chancellor himself. During its sixteen years the University's academic staff published over 2,200 books and articles and secured research grants from external sources totalling over £4m. In 1981 the University's Industrial Unit was established with a grant of £70,000 from the Wolfson Foundation. The unit provided a focus for consultancy work and was a highly effective interface between the University and the world of industry.

A NEW APPROACH AT MAGEE

The Institute of Continuing Education was established at Magee in 1972, following the Senate's decision to discontinue undergraduate teaching at the College. The Council approved the advertisement of an initial eighteen academic posts, including those of Director and four professorial heads of division. Staff at the Institute organised a wide range of short courses, conferences and extra mural studies; they also delivered in-service courses and a number of award-bearing postgraduate courses, including the MA in Continuing Education and the Diploma in Advanced Studies in Education. Extra-mural courses were offered in twelve locations across Northern Ireland. Other professors who were at the Institute included Steve Badley, head of Public Administration, and Reggie Smith, the husband of the novelist Olivia Manning, and the inspiration for the character of Guy Pringle in her Balkan and Levant trilogies. Professor Rex Cathcart came to the Institute from working in television. A producer of acclaimed radio and television documentaries, he later published a history of the BBC in Northern Ireland, *A Most Contrary Region*. The development of the Institute was inhibited by the unsettled conditions experienced in Derry throughout the 1970s. Nearby terrorist activity, particularly in the evenings and at night, made many potential students reluctant to cross the Craigavon Bridge to attend classes. For staff and students

17 The library at Magee in the late 1960s.

evening journeys to Magee were occasionally accompanied by sounds of gunfire.

The Institute offered a successful Nurse Tutor's programme and established a Community Education Resource Centre for the use of voluntary groups. The Community Studies Division, headed by Professor Derek Carter, offered courses in professional development, particularly for social workers. In 1974 the first province-wide conference for community development workers was held at Magee. Organised by Tom Lovett, this led to the establishment of a cross-community association of community workers known as Community Organisation Northern Ireland (CONI) and to a major action research project, the Community Action, Research and Education (CARE) project.

The Certificate in Foundation Studies for Mature Students was an imaginative attempt to meet the needs of disadvantaged adults and became the precursor of many similar courses throughout the United Kingdom. Pioneered by Frank D'Arcy, it began in 1973 with nine full-time and three part-time students. Six years later, with substantial funding from the Department of Education, full-time student numbers had risen to forty each year with a further sixty part-timers studying across two years. Of all the innovations of these years the emergence of this 'access course', as it came to be known, was a highly significant contribution to developments across the entire university sector.

In the event, nevertheless, NUU's efforts to develop Magee were judged to be inadequate. The outcome of its efforts fell short of what everyone wished to see. Indeed for many, the removal of under-graduate studies from Magee and their replacement by Continuing Education courses, appeared to cast doubt on the College's university status. The newly merged University of Ulster addressed the deficit with fresh energy and considerable imagination, re-introducing undergraduate studies and a broad range of postgraduate courses. Using substantial additional resources of its own as well as those provided by government, it accorded the highest priority to the development of Magee, with major and permanent results.

STUDENT LIFE AT NUU

What was it like to be a student at a young university on the north Atlantic coast of Northern Ireland? Lindsay McKeon, an NUU graduate in Psychology from the 1970s, has provided some impressions of her time as a student at Coleraine:

> a real engagement with my subject; a wonderful sense of community within the university; lots of interest in developing and sharing new ideas; the modular nature of the course gave one a deep introduction to many applied fields; seminar groups were too small for one to be invisible and hide; fantastic support for intervarsity exchange in all sports; being generously funded to go fencing; interacting with really interesting people like playwright Frank McGuinness; PhD students sharing about their ideas and work; the Riverside Theatre; interdepartmental indoor mixed football; a commitment to quality.[11]

11 Personal communication to the author, May 2007.

18 The Coleraine campus in the mid-1970s.

She draws attention to key features of student life at Coleraine and points out that students and staff enjoyed some benefits from the University's difficulties in recruiting additional students. Physical facilities were spacious and well appointed. The campus was relatively compact and intimate, and developed a largely informal and close-knit community, exemplifying the kind of academic and social setting that many of today's universities strive to achieve. The Riverside Theatre, other cultural activities, and high staff and student participation rates in sport and recreation provided compensation to some degree for the University's geographical remoteness. The University as a whole was a remarkably unhierarchical institution and the relative isolation of the Coleraine area, and of the campus, encouraged a community ethos. The academic system, with its strong degree of interdisciplinarity, furthered this, as did the physical organisation of the campus, which had been specifically designed to promote integration.

THE DÉNOUEMENT AND THE LEGACY

In the late summer of 1976 the first Vice-Chancellor, Professor Alan Burges, retired. His successor was Wilfred Cockcroft, formerly Professor of Mathematics at Hull and a member of the University Grants Committee. Dr Cockcroft had been in office for only a few months when the Public Accounts Committee of the House of Commons strongly criticised the University Grants Committee for its policy toward the New University of Ulster. The Comptroller and Auditor General had conducted a review of the use of space in the buildings at Coleraine and examined the University Grants Committee's financial policy towards the University. The Public Accounts Committee called on the Department of Education to provide an explanation for the failure of the University to achieve its targets for student numbers.

The Department's response was formulated following conversations with the University authorities and suggested two main reasons for the shortfall in numbers. These were, firstly, a sudden and unpredicted (though in fact short-lived) decline in the demand for higher education throughout the United Kingdom, and secondly, and in particular, the effect of Northern Ireland's 'Troubles'. The political violence had not only made universities in Great Britain more attractive to students from Northern Ireland but had discouraged any significant influx of students from outside the province. The response might also have mentioned other factors, such as the lack of any effective mechanism in the Department of Education for planning higher education and the rapid and unanticipated growth of under-graduate degree studies at the Ulster Polytechnic (as it was by now known), at Jordanstown, The growth of the Polytechnic was not restricted by the quinquennial planning system imposed on universities by the University Grants Committee. This had led to competition for undergraduate students between the three institutions in Northern Ireland. A further perspective which failed to find its way into the Department's response was the fact that the Northern Ireland government had accepted Lockwood's speculative student number targets for the New University, while rejecting the Committee's key recommendation regarding the establishment of a foundational Faculty of Agriculture.

In August 1978 Roy Mason, Secretary of State for Northern Ireland, announced his decision to establish an independent review of higher education in Northern Ireland to be chaired by Sir Henry Chilver of Cranfield Institute of Technology. The Chilver Committee deliberated for three-and-a-half years. In 1980 it produced an interim report about rationalising teacher education (which engendered fierce controversy, and alienated Northern Ireland's churches, and which the government was unable to implement). Sir Henry's final Report was published by the Department of Education on 23 March 1982. The Report astonished and disappointed many of the academics and administrative staff of NUU who considered that Chilver's account of the record of the University was shallow and dismissive. The Committee's recommendations were thought to be bizarre and unworthy of a major committee chaired by an eminent educationalist. These recommendations included an increased involvement with mature students, a greater emphasis on activities relevant to the needs of the Northern Ireland community and the development of distance learning. These were measures which, the Report acknowledged, would amount to a scaling down of the work of the University. Chilver admitted that 'the resulting institution might well be some-what smaller in terms of total enrolments than is the present NUU but ... we believe that it would be academically viable'.[12]

What most incensed the University's Council and Senate, however, was the Report's lack of analysis of higher education needs in Northern Ireland, coupled with its disparaging attitude to the University. The University's substantial research achievements were dismissed in a mere eleven lines and its contribution to the wider Northern Ireland community was criticised and undervalued. Commenting on the Report, the Vice-Chancellor drew attention to the 'many errors of fact and interpretation which litter it' and maintained that 'many of the assertions in the report are quite untenable and are based on misinterpretations and misunderstandings which are surprising – and in my view ... disgraceful in a report of this importance'.[13] Chilver had toiled long and produced little. Derek

12 *The Future of Higher Education in Northern Ireland*, (1982), [Final Report of the Higher Education Review Group chaired by Sir Henry Chilver], para. 1.14, 5. 13 Writing in a special edition of the University's *Bulletin*, 22 April 1982, 1.

19 The Coleraine campus in the 1980s.

Birley, Rector of the Ulster Polytechnic, described Chilver's prescription as 'a gallimaufry ... without coherence'. Students in such an institution would be pursuing a 'motley assortment of disparate courses', and would be 'as miscellaneous a bunch as you would hope to find in a day's march'. The proposals, if implemented, would result in a 'very puny liberal arts college'.[14]

On 23 March all of Chilver's main recommendations were comprehensively rejected by the Government which, ninety minutes after the release of the Report, published a White Paper, *The Future Structure of Higher Education in Northern Ireland*, outlining its decision that the New University of Ulster would merge with the Ulster Polytechnic to form a new university-level institution.

The University brought as its dowry to this academic and institutional marriage with the Ulster Polytechnic a range of assets,

14 A.P. Williamson, 'The New University of Ulster, 1965–1984: A Chapter in University State Relations in Northern Ireland' (PhD, University of Dublin, 1988) 307.

intellectual, physical and symbolic, which were to play their part in the future development of the University of Ulster. These included highly qualified staff and rigorous academic standards and traditions, together with well-stocked libraries and a strong research reputation in the physical, biological and social sciences and the humanities. To this should be added groundbreaking work in teacher education and in adult and continuing education. The extensive campus at Coleraine and the buildings and grounds at Magee College provided well-endowed facilities for the future. NUU had fostered interdisciplinary studies; and had gained extensive experience of managing a semester system which, with some additions, was soon to become the norm throughout the university system in the United Kingdom. The Riverside Theatre at Coleraine was, and continues to be, a major cultural resource for the northern part of Northern Ireland. As a visual symbol of continuity, NUU's academic colours and grant of arms were adopted by the University of Ulster and its Chancellor, Lord Grey, became the first Chancellor of the merged institution. Upon these foundations, together with those of the Ulster Polytechnic, a major university was created.

   The words 'To Build Anew' provided the legend of the Grant of Arms of both the New University of Ulster and of the University of Ulster. They were taken from a poem by W.B. Yeats, 'The Rose in the Deeps of His Heart.' The merger offered an opportunity 'to build anew'. In this regard Lockwood's original vision was remarkably prescient. He wished Northern Ireland to have a university comprehending all. After twenty-five years the University of Ulster, as the United Kingdom's first transbinary university, has realised, and greatly exceeded, Lockwood's aspiration for the people of Northern Ireland.

4

Ulster College to Ulster Polytechnic

DON McCLOY

'There is no reason for complacency. We have come together and this complex organisation works, which is no mean achievement. But this is the beginning, and to continue to be effective we must strive always to do better ... The visionary gleam is still in our eyes, never long dimmed by mishap or discouragement, and our horizons are therefore still as far away as ever.'[1]

BEGINNINGS

The Lockwood Report's hierarchical approach gave relatively low priority to the proposed Ulster College. Only three of its seventy main recommendations and eight of its 130 pages were devoted to the College, and five of the latter were concerned solely with the training of technicians. However, despite the sketchy nature of the proposal, government was taken with the idea of a new College. The related recommendations, which confirmed the Ministry's view that there was a need (as in England and Wales) for better co-ordination of further education, were accepted. A new Regional College of Technology and the existing Colleges of Art and of Domestic Science in Belfast would together provide the initial building blocks of the new Ulster College. It would serve the whole of Northern Ireland and

1 D.S. Birley, 'Report to Governors', March 1974; 'Annual Report to Governors', August 1974. Much background material has been gathered from minutes of the Board of Governors, and from Director's reports to Governors – all available in the University of Ulster's archive at Coleraine. The author has also been able to refer to a substantial number of private communications to him from Mr Birley. In addition, he acknowledges the wealth of helpful information and statistical data provided in the Lockwood Report (*Higher Education in Northern Ireland*, 1965); Chilver's Final Report (The Future of Higher Education in Northern Ireland, 1982; the *House of Commons Report on Further and Higher Education in Northern Ireland*, 1982; and the Polytechnic's formal submission to Chilver ('A Profile Prepared for the Higher Education Review Group', February, 1979).

provide high-level, non-degree courses across a wide range of disciplines. It would be governed by an independent Board, appointments to which would have regard 'for the educational well-being of the College rather than to political, professional and other extraneous considerations'.[2] It would be financed by direct grants, both capital and recurrent, from the Ministry of Education.

The Lockwood Report also recommended that, in the long term, all the constituent colleges should be based on a common campus, thereby facilitating 'the intermingling of staff and the sharing by students of common amenities and activities such as characterise a university'.[3] The acquisition of a suitable site, a complicated task, was the first practical step towards the implementation of this grand scheme. The Ministry had envisaged advantages – such as the sharing of resources and the articulation of courses –in a close association between the Ulster College and the Queen's University of Belfast (QUB), so when searches for a site began in the Spring of 1965, they were concentrated on the central Belfast area. This was a fruitless exercise, however. The search had to be extended and, after considering a number of sites close to the city, it was decided that eighty-two acres of land at Sunnyside, Jordanstown, some eight miles from the city, were suitable. The site was acquired, on behalf of the Ministry, by Vesting Order in September 1967. By happy coincidence, it abutted on the thirty-two acre campus of the Ulster College of Physical Education (UCPE) – a small College which had not found a place in Lockwood's scheme of things. The Ministry now added UCPE to Ulster College's component parts.

Planning gradually gathered momentum. Priority was given to the new Regional College of Technology since its potential offerings were considered to be urgently required in the educational, industrial and economic interests of Northern Ireland. Preliminary schedules of courses and accommodation were drawn up in early 1966 by a Working Party consisting of representatives of the Ministry of Education and the Belfast Education Authority, along with staff from the Belfast College of Technology. Their recommendations were submitted to the Ministry in April 1966 and after some deliberation it was decided to appoint Lord Jackson of Burnley, a member of the Lockwood Committee, as consultant to the project.

2 *Lockwood Report*, 99.   3 *Lockwood Report*, 98.

Legal matters slowed progress. Legislation was required to provide for the transfer to the Ministry of Education, firstly, of the Colleges of Art and Domestic Science from the Belfast Corporation; secondly, of the Ulster College of Physical Education from the Ministry of Finance; and finally of the eighty-two acre site at Jordanstown from the Belfast Corporation. The establishment of a Board of Governors and the means of grant payment to that Board also required legislation. All these issues were addressed in the Ulster College Bill, which was placed before the House of Commons in April 1968 and received Royal Assent on 4 July 1968.

GOVERNORS IN CONTROL

It was becoming abundantly clear that the proposed College needed champions to drive matters forward. Those champions, the Governors, had just been appointed and held their first formal meeting on 16 July 1969. They were assuming a daunting set of responsibilities, but they were independent and could, 'subject to such directions, if any, as the Minister may give, determine the courses to be provided in the College'.[4] The first, indeed the only, Chairman of the Board of Governors was W.A. McNeill, a distinguished local businessman.

The first meeting gave the Governors an opportunity to display their resolve and independence. Their first action was to establish a Steering Committee to consider and process information on relevant matters for presentation to the full Board. But they were taken aback when, under 'Any Other Business', John Benn, the Permanent Secretary, raised the question of inspection. Members objected to the introduction of such an important matter so late in the agenda and, when the issue re-surfaced at the September meeting of the Steering Committee, the Governors stood firm, maintaining that 'inspection would greatly debase the status of the Ulster College which ought to be regarded as an institution in the sphere of higher education of equivalent standing to [a] university'.[5]

The Governors were acutely aware of the many changes that had taken place in higher education 'across the water' since the publication of the Lockwood Report in 1965. A binary system of universities and

4 'Ulster College Regulations', 1969.   5 'Minutes of the Steering Committee of the Board of Governors', 19 September 1969.

public sector polytechnics had been established, with degrees in the latter validated and awarded by a Council for National and Academic Awards (CNAA). So the Governors soon expressed doubts about the restricted range and level of the courses which Lockwood had envisaged for Ulster College. Lord Jackson informed them at their second meeting, in October 1969, that the major concern of the College should be with the status and supply of engineering technicians. Recognising 'the limited attraction this would have for the staff of the College of Technology, who would always be hoping for degree work',[6] he feared that any move towards degrees would undermine provision for technicians; and, if such a move were made, degrees should be sponsored by the local universities, not by the CNAA. The Governors voiced their concerns that such policies would place Ulster College in a position inferior to the universities.

The CNAA was helping to raise the status of the polytechnics in Great Britain and, with the College having all the attributes of a polytechnic, an association with the CNAA seemed the next logical step in its development. The Governors found it difficult to see how an institution, offering HNDs and advanced courses, could avoid proceeding to offer degree courses: but, reluctant to disturb traditional hierarchies, the Ministry was opposed to any such development.

HIERARCHY CHALLENGED

The appointment of a Director in the Spring of 1970 re-opened the debate. Derek Sydney Birley, a Yorkshireman and former Education Officer, had clear views on the way ahead. He strongly supported the Governors' view that the College should have the freedom to help its students reach their full potential. If degrees were needed, they should be provided.

One degree, at least, seemed certain to grace the College's prospectus – the QUB degree in Pharmacy, run by the Belfast College of Technology (BCT), and expected to transfer to the Ulster College along with other advanced courses. The assumption that the degree in Pharmacy would move to Jordanstown, whilst still under the control of QUB, was soon tested. On 23 March 1970 the Governors' Steering Committee was advised that a problem had arisen concerning the

6 'Minutes of the Board of Governors', 16 October 1969.

placing of Pharmacy and Applied Chemistry courses between the Queen's University and Ulster College. Based largely on an argument that students did not want to move to Jordanstown, the University opposed the transfer. Three Governors, including the Director-designate, were nominated to discuss the issue with the Vice-Chancellor and his colleagues on 14 April 1970. Surprising to some, the College representatives agreed to yield up the course – albeit on two conditions: the College should not be penalised financially because of the extra resources required by QUB; and of greater strategic importance, it was to be clearly understood that withdrawal of the course would fundamentally change the relationship that Lockwood had envisaged between QUB and Ulster College. Trust had been undermined, and the College's fears of loss of freedom and sub-servience to QUB had been confirmed. The latter of these two conditions was the critical one, opening the door to a long and fruitful interaction with the CNAA.

'E PLURIBUS UNUM'

The organisation of Ulster College was a crucial matter. If it proceeded as a collection of disparate colleges, the likelihood of any real innovation would be reduced considerably. New developments, other than those achieved by the original colleges themselves, were unlikely. Interactions had to be built in from the start.

There was a danger, however, that loosely-formed interactions, based on wishful thinking, would be merely cosmetic with little prospect of any real benefit to students and the community. The Director's first report to the Governors proposed a scheme which would facilitate, and require, fruitful interaction across the spectrum of the College's academic and corporate activity. Faculties were pro-posed, cutting across the administrative boundaries of the constituent colleges. Led by full-time Deans, the Faculties would be concerned, in the main, with academic development, leaving the various colleges to focus on pastoral, social, domestic and recreational matters. The Director argued that this device would help to develop a coherent philosophy for the new venture; it would encourage and facilitate the development of interdisciplinary programmes of study; it would make optimum use of scarce teaching staff; and it would provide ample opportunity for staff to mix on professional as well as social grounds.

The Governors agreed with the proposal and to the establishment of six Faculties – Arts, Commerce & Management, Education, Social Sciences, Science, and Technology.

The Director's first report also argued that the title of the new institution had an important bearing on its ethos, reputation and effectiveness. There was terminological confusion, in that the entity was designated a college whilst its constituent elements were themselves colleges; while, to compound matters, two of the colleges had 'Ulster' in their title. The major concern about terminology, however, was the Governors' belief that the name of the new institution should clearly reflect its purpose: to offer, to the highest levels and across the spectrum from arts to sciences, a complete range of courses relevant to contemporary life. In Great Britain such institutions were called polytechnics. Why not the Ulster Polytechnic? The Governors agreed that such a change would give their charge a point of reference within the existing British system of higher education; and that the new identity would assist the process of integration and foster the recruitment of staff and students.

While the logic behind the proposed change seemed unassailable, the Ministry concluded that it would be too radical and too soon. However, solid progress was made when the Governors' alternative proposal was adopted. The descriptive phrase 'the Northern Ireland Polytechnic' would be used after 'Ulster College'; and 'Polytechnic' would be used in all correspondence, internal memoranda and other literature as a general description, distinguishing the institution as a whole from its constituent colleges. The new title did not become legal until March 1975 but, by then, the man in the street was well aware of the Polytechnic, its offerings and its whereabouts. The College was formally re-designated Ulster Polytechnic in 1978.

MEETING NEEDS

Whilst the immediate needs of the embryonic College were matters of great concern, everyone recognised that priority had to be given to those it was designed to serve – students, industry, business and the community. The Academic Board, which began its formal work in 1971, recognised and attempted to define the various conflicting demands likely to arise. Students, for example, might prefer flexible courses with interdisciplinary content, leading to a range of career opportunities. Industry and the professions, on the other hand, were likely to want sharply-focused programmes. Recognition of such tensions and the will to resolve them were demonstrated in the Academic Board's plans to promote learning through full-time and part-time courses, and through research; to co-operate with industry and commerce; and to serve the wider community.

Courses of study would provide the major means of delivering these plans. Every new course, and every existing one, was to be scrutinised against seven criteria, of which evidence of demand from potential students and of need – professional, industrial or social – were paramount. The concepts of relevance and flexibility also attracted special attention, becoming guiding principles, giving a special stamp to the Polytechnic's courses and helping to shape its ethos. The concept of relevance created some tensions – relevance to whom or to what? Should courses be relevant in the sense of meeting professional, industrial or social needs? Or in the sense of meeting student demand? A balance had to be struck between need and demand.

As far as need was concerned it was recognised that students had to be prepared for the real world. Courses should be responsive to the needs of professional bodies and employers, and the identification of these needs required close collaboration with the professions and with the world of work. The Polytechnic worked hard on many fronts to achieve that collaboration: practitioners were invited to contribute to course design and delivery; site visits and case-studies became standard practice; student projects were focused on employers' needs. Sandwich courses, linking theory and practice, provided an ideal means of collaboration. Many three-year diploma courses required students to spend the middle year in industry, and most four-year degrees used the penultimate year similarly. The 'year out' required careful planning if it was to contribute adequately to the student's development and to the company's needs. This was no mean feat; indeed, the sandwich principle had earlier been abandoned at the College of Technology because of difficulties in securing satisfactory placements. Nevertheless, Polytechnic staff pursued the policy vigorously and the numbers of students placed each year grew steadily. In 1980–1 some 296 full-time students were attached to industry for six months and a further 267 for a full academic year.

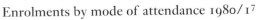

Enrolments by mode of attendance 1980/1[7]

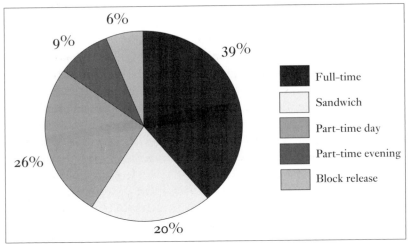

6%

9%

39%

26%

20%

Full-time

Sandwich

Part-time day

Part-time evening

Block release

Flexibility in course provision helped to bridge the gap between student demand and employer need. The Polytechnic would not be a self-serving institution. Programmes of study would be designed to meet the needs of students and employers – not the convenience of the institution. Several different methods of course delivery were deployed. Employers could release their staff to attend part-time courses for a few hours during day or evening, or for 'blocks' of up to twelve weeks at a time. Courses ranged from three-year Higher National Certificates (HNCs) to one-day updating specialisms for practising professionals. By 1978–9 part-time enrolments had grown to some 3,500. The practical experience of these people, and their maturity, brought valuable insights to fellow students and did much to bridge the gap between theory and practice.

Flexibility was not only evident in mode of attendance; its pursuit also affected course content. Where possible, courses were designed to prepare students for rewarding careers and not solely for specific jobs. This led to increasing interaction among the various Faculties and much effort was devoted to crossing the traditional boundaries between disciplines. With the vicissitudes of the market place and the abundant evidence of the shortcomings of manpower planning in mind, broadly-based programmes with delayed vocational choice through late specialisation were pursued as the ideal.

7 *Ulster Polytechnic 10th Anniversary*, 1981.

The quest for flexibility placed students at the centre of planning. Patterns of interrelating courses at different levels were created to provide ladders of opportunity allowing students to reach their optimal capability, and simultaneously to provide safety nets for those whose reach exceeded their grasp. This philosophy was clearly demonstrated in the interactions between Higher National Diplomas (HNDs) and degrees, in which the more able diploma students had opportunities to transfer to degree courses, and those struggling with degree studies could transfer to diplomas. However, whilst pedagogically sound, this approach to course design was not always easily reconciled with the rigid hierarchical structures of some professional bodies.

The Polytechnic's growing expertise in course development cannot be overstated. Staff developed an understanding of the pedagogical potential of evolving knowledge bases in subjects like Computing, and were able to create new courses, and to adjust existing ones, accordingly. Through their close contacts with practitioners, staff soon became expert in identifying the training needs of evolving professional areas. They had to imagine the shape and outcome of new and amended programmes and justify them to validation panels. And as changing market conditions counselled the replacement of certificate by diploma courses, and diplomas by degrees, staff were obliged to refresh and upgrade their own knowledge of the various fields. The process of validation, both internal and external, could be a harrowing experience, and there was much celebration when a course team managed to satisfy an aggressive team of inquisitors, whether from the CNAA or elsewhere. The process did much to raise institutional morale and to maintain a vibrant *esprit de corps*.

BRICKS, MORTAR AND MONEY

The semi-rural nature of the Jordanstown site posed problems for the architects. Development of the whole site involved considerations of car-parking and of student accommodation. A comprehensive plan eventually found its way to the Ministry of Education in October 1968, but approval was restricted to the first phase of the Regional College, where accommodation had been based on the assumed transfer of advanced courses from the Belfast Colleges of Technology and Business. The project went to tender in the autumn of 1969 and Building Design Partnership was chosen to take it forward.

20 Main buildings at Jordanstown in the 1970s.

The first phase of the new buildings at Jordanstown provided lecture rooms and laboratories for Science in Blocks 1, 2 and 7, and communal and administrative accommodation in Blocks 8 and 9. Courses commenced in somewhat chaotic and dusty conditions in September 1971. Phase 2, completed the following year, provided buildings for Technology and for Business Administration & Management in Blocks 3, 4 and 5, along with an Assembly Hall (Block 10) and a Sports Hall. Financial constraints placed further development in some jeopardy, but a favourable wind soon blew across the campus. Published in January 1973, the Cairncross Report aimed to reduce unemployment in the province by increasing public spending. Ulster College's capital development plan was allocated £3.5 million of this windfall, and Phase 3 of its building programme went ahead with gusto. Between 1974 and 1977 Blocks 12 and 14 provided much needed accommodation for Education, Humanities and Social and Health Sciences. A splendid Library was established in Block 13, and Block 11 included sports halls and other recreational

21 Ulster College: part of the student village.

facilities and housed the Students' Union. Block 15, for the Faculties of Business Administration and Education, became operational in 1977. By 1978 some £10.5 million had been spent on new build, and there was more to come. Block 18 followed in 1980, but Block 16, planned to house the Art and Design Schools on transfer from Belfast, was not to materialise within the life-span of the Polytechnic. Whilst the Department of Education (DENI became responsible for all levels of education in 1975) had approved the move in principle, it was concerned about the relative newness of the York Street building and felt that the transfer might generate only marginal increases in student numbers. A massive development of student residences was among the Governors' major achievements. Government's initial plans had not contemplated the need for any such provision, but by 1980 the Governors' persistence in the matter had generated some 800 residential places in student halls, chalets and a student village.

Capital requirements were crucial, but recurrent monies – keeping the show on the road – were equally important. Total recurrent

income grew from £6.099 million in 1975–6 to £11.058 million in
1979–80. Delays in the approval of estimates caused the Director
some early anguish, but mutual respect between the Polytechnic and
the Department was soon established. The rigour of the Finance
Committee, and the diligence of the Finance Officer and his team,
generated growing confidence in the Polytechnic's estimates and its
system of financial controls. Cost-effectiveness was most evident in
costs-per-student. The Polytechnic's submission to Chilver sought to
demonstrate that these were substantially lower than those of the two
universities.

SETTING OUT THE STALL

The first few years of the new institution were a testing time. Would
paper plans translate into concrete reality? Would the concepts of
inter-professional training and delayed choice begin to take on
substance? Would the Polytechnic's characteristic interdisciplinary
approach prove effective?

The Colleges of Art, Domestic Science and Physical Education
were formally subsumed within the Ulster College on 1 April 1971
and the transferred courses were advertised under the banner of the
new institution. Advertising was a relatively easy task, but delivery was
a different story altogether. Many feared that the new Phase 1
buildings would not be ready for a September start, but nerves held
and staff breathed a sigh of relief when the first students arrived in
the autumn of 1971. Amounting to some 1,500 full-time equivalents,
the first intakes at Jordanstown settled down to their studies
apparently unconcerned by the dust and debris surrounding them.
The Phase 1 buildings housed Science courses and some marine-
related areas of Technology. The large majority of students had been
transferred from elsewhere, but a sprinkling of new ones encouraged
staff and governors alike.

The new Faculties were beginning to show their mettle, with
Scientists in the vanguard. Delays in the completion of Phase 1
buildings caused Science courses to be launched under unsatisfactory
conditions; in some cases the unfinished state of laboratories required
practical work to be deferred until late in the year. Undaunted,
students and staff applied themselves to a comprehensive portfolio of
courses. A highlight, of great significance to the future development

of the Polytechnic, was the CNAA's approval of a BSc Combined Sciences. Its recognition informed the world at large that the Polytechnic was a credible institution.

There were many other early and effective responses. For example, the Faculty of Arts soon gained recognition at the highest level. Staff were convinced that the new national qualification, the Diploma in Art and Design, pitched at degree level, had much to offer. So there was delight and pride when their bid to run such programmes received resounding approbation in 1972 from the National Council for Diplomas in Art and Design (NCDAD). These diplomas were re-designated nationally as degrees (BAs) when the CNAA and the NCDAD amalgamated in 1974.

The Faculty of Education also had its early successes. At the outset it had to assume responsibility for the training of secondary and further education teachers in five areas; Physical Education – originating in the Ulster College of Physical Education; Domestic Science and Catering – from the Belfast College of Domestic Science; Art – from the Ulster College of Art and Design; and Heavy Crafts – from the Belfast College of Technology (BCT). This complex amalgamation was completed within a year. A comprehensive re-design of the then existing three-year diplomas ensured that theory and practice were linked. This restructuring was carried through to degree level, and a CNAA BEd degree found its way onto the Polytechnic's books in 1973.

New accommodation for the Faculty of Management and Commerce, shortly to be re-named Business Administration, was not available until 1972, so the year 1971–2 was largely devoted to planning. A start was made on the re-design of the several HNCs and HNDs which were to transfer from other colleges. And new courses were planned, including HNCs in Police Studies and Business Studies, HNDs in Institutional Management and Hotel & Catering Administration, as well as a range of professional courses in Accountancy, Insurance and Management. A highlight was the September 1973 launch of a BA degree in Business Studies.

An internal organisational review saw the early transfer of the Humanities component of the Faculty of Social Sciences and Humanities to the Faculty of Arts. The inclusion of the Social Sciences and the Humanities as discrete disciplines in the portfolio of the new institution surprised some. Lockwood had not envisaged such a development, but the Polytechnic's Governors were convinced that

22 Line drawing of the library at Jordanstown.

the Humanities had much more to offer than the provision of a liberal studies dimension in other Polytechnic programmes. A welcome boost to confidence was the decision by the Ministry of Health and Social Services to negotiate the transfer of the Northern Ireland School of Physiotherapy to the Polytechnic. The entire teaching staff, along with 103 students, moved to Jordanstown in January 1972. The Ministry also agreed to support the establishment, for the first time in Northern Ireland, of a course in Occupational Therapy.

Lack of accommodation restricted the Faculty of Technology's offerings at Jordanstown in 1971 to a few courses in Navigation and Marine Electronics. However, there was much to be done on the planning front. HNCs and HNDs transferring from the BCT were revised to include a sandwich year, and a complementary CNAA BSc in Engineering commenced in 1974. All this required the advice and commitment of practitioners. The professions gave active encouragement. The Royal Institution of Chartered Surveyors, for example, and

1 The original buildings at Magee College.

2 The Steering Group for the merger: Sir Peter Swinnerton–Dyer, Chairman (*front row centre*) and Sir Norman Lindop, Vice-Chairman (*to his left*).

3 The ceremonial mace of the University of Ulster. Designed,
constructed and engraved by Mr Mike McCrory, former
Head of the School of Fine and Applied Art.

4a The Belfast campus from the air, 2001.

4b The Coleraine campus from the air, 2001.

the local branches of the Institution of Quantity Surveyors supported the launch of the first full-time surveying course in Northern Ireland – a four-year sandwich diploma with a first year common to both quantity surveyors and general practice surveyors.

All these developments took place against a background of political volatility and intense civil unrest, which 'had a shrivelling effect on many things inside the Polytechnic as well as out'.[8] In March 1972 a NCDAD visiting party to the College of Art found the Belfast campus sealed off by security forces. Indeed, most validating bodies found great difficulty persuading panel members to visit Northern Ireland and this required, for example, Ulster College staff to travel to London for CNAA validations of their courses. There were further distractions when the Workers' Council strike of May 1974 disrupted examinations as well as forcing the liquidation of the firm contracted to build the new student village. And there was physical damage. In 1971 the College of Art and its out-centre at Hope Street suffered severe bomb damage. But the worst atrocities were to follow in 1977 and 1983 when bombs at Jordanstown injured many and caused the deaths of three policemen. This was a trying time for the new institution, but it stood firm as the creator of something new in the midst of rampant destruction.

GROWTH AND MATURITY

A spirit of adventure drove the Polytechnic forward. Optimism grew as students flocked to the various courses. In only its second year the new institution's enrolment exceeded 2,500, a figure well in excess of anything envisaged by Lockwood. By 1973–4 some 174 courses were on offer; 71 full-time and sandwich, and 103 part-time. Twelve new degree courses were running, and there were 26 new high-level certificates and diplomas ranging from Music to Occupational Therapy, from the education of retarded children to Civil Engineering. The six Faculties soon evolved into effective engines of innovation and delivery, and by 1978 they had grown to include 36 Schools and Divisions. In addition, two Centres – Management Education and Continuing Education – added to the impressive array of expertise.

8 D.S. Birley, private communication to the author.

Enrolments by Faculty and Centre[9]

FACULTY/CENTRE	1972/3	1975/6	1978/9
Arts	679	1032	1157
Business Administration	949	1377	1697
Education	539	543	683
Management & Continuing Education	–	285	358
Science	451	630	770
Social & Health Sciences	257	653	1013
Technology	1054	1460	1768
TOTAL	3929	5980	7446

By any standards the growth in the number and variety of courses at the Polytechnic was remarkable. This was no matter of chance. The Academic Board had been quick to recognise the importance of co-ordinated planning and quality control. Its Course Development Group (later the Development Committee) and the Academic Programmes Committee were charged with initiating and implementing a system of scrutiny. By 1978 over 40 new teaching programmes had been designed and launched. In 1981, in view of the evident rigour of the new system, the Chilver Committee saw 'no objection in principle to a change to self-validation by the Polytechnic if the balance of practical advantage appeared to shift in this direction'.[10]

By the end of its first decade the Polytechnic's courses had settled into four fairly distinct categories: those leading to degrees; to professional qualifications; to certificates and diplomas; and continuing education courses.

Degree programmes developed rapidly. In 1975–6 some 29 per cent of the Polytechnic's students were studying at degree level or higher, but this grew to 54 per cent by 1980–1, a figure which was, coincidentally, identical to the average in the 30 English and Welsh Polytechnics. Growth was driven by the demands of students and the professions. The Chilver Committee acknowledged the need for this provision: 'the extent and pace of this growth are remarkable by any

9 'A Profile Prepared for the Higher Education Review Group', 51, Ulster Polytechnic, February 1979. 10 Chilver's *Final Report*, 93.

Enrolments 1971/2 to 1980/1[11]

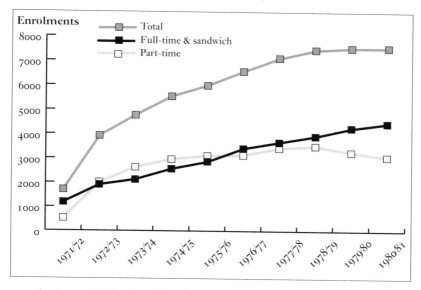

standards, and it is clear that the courses provided by the Polytechnic have matched well with the needs and desires of Northern Ireland students'.[12]

Percentage distribution of students by level of study: Ulster Polytechnic compared with Polytechnics in England and Wales[13]

	1975–6		1980–1	
	Ulster	Eng/Wales	Ulster	Eng/Wales
Higher Degrees	0.8	1.3	1.7	1.6
Other Postgraduate	9.7	9.0	10.0	5.6
First Degrees	18.6	33.7	42.4	46.9
Other Higher Education	54.8	45.4	35.1	35.9
Other	16.1	10.6	10.8	10.0

11 Data to 1979 from 'A Profile Prepared for the Higher Education Review Group'; from 1979 to 1981 from *Ulster Polytechnic 10th Anniversary*. 12 Chilver's *Final Report*, 91. 13 Chilver's *Final Report*, 165, 166.

The changing requirements of professional bodies also had their impact. In the Faculty of Education, for example, the original diploma provision had to be re-designed in response to the national policy on an 'all-graduate' teaching profession.

As an important centre for vocational education, the Polytechnic had to establish close and effective relations with the professions from the very outset. Whilst exemptions provided by many courses helped students along the road to professional status, a more direct way of achieving the same end was through courses which prepared students for professional examinations. These latter covered a wide spectrum of disciplines, including preparation for the examinations of the Society of Dyers and Colourists, and for the Council of the Engineering Institutions. And they were at differing levels – some were considered equivalent to ordinary degrees, and some to honours. By 1978 some 26 advanced courses of this nature were on offer, some part-time, some full-time.

Certificates and diplomas were offered in abundance at various levels, including postgraduate. Some were the Polytechnic's own offerings: in the profession of Surveying, for example, part-time programmes had traditionally prepared students for the examinations of the Royal Institute of Chartered Surveyors (RICS), but the Polytechnic led the change from part-time to full-time study in 1973. And there was further change in 1976 when the RICS endorsed the Polytechnic's new four-year sandwich Diplomas in Quantity Surveying and General Practice Surveying, and granted graduates exemption from professional examinations.

A significant number of courses at certificate and diploma levels fell under the aegis of national bodies such as the CNAA, the Business Education Council (BEC) and the Technician Education Council (TEC). The several diplomas in the arts were initially offered on behalf of the NCDAD, and, for example, the part-time Certificate in Education (Further Education) was a CNAA award, as was the Postgraduate Diploma in Management Studies (DMS). A recognised educational requirement for Associate Membership of the British Institute of Management (BIM), the DMS became one of the more popular offerings of the Centre for Management Education. The establishment of BEC and TEC in the late 1970s, and the merged Business and Technical Education Council (BTEC) in 1983, helped guide the development of the HNCs and HNDs (later HCs and HDs) which formed a crucial component of the Polytechnic's portfolio. By

1981 the range of HNDs had been comprehensively extended with the introduction of 12 new programmes. Over 900 students were pursuing these full-time and sandwich programmes, with another 700 on a wide range of part-time HNCs.

The Academic Board recognised that education was truly a lifelong affair. Rapid changes in society, in technology, in the professions and in leisure were generating needs and demands for continuing education – from cradle to grave. Whilst the various Faculties could respond in their different ways to these needs, the Academic Board feared that they might, by default, get low priority as Faculties worked hard to establish their portfolios of certificated courses. The Centre for Continuing Education was established to raise the profile of such activities and to support and encourage Faculties in their delivery. In addition to its coordinating and promotional role, the Centre also developed its own courses. The number of short courses and related students grew respectively from 97 to 137, and from 1,993 to 3,016 between 1978 and 1981.

EXTENDING AND APPLYING KNOWLEDGE

From the outset the Academic Board acknowledged the important roles that research and staff development might play in improving the quality of teaching programmes. The Awards, Research and Consultancy Committee (ARCC) was charged with the development of policies designed to promote and regulate research, consultancy and related activities. What research would be most appropriate to the Polytechnic, to its skills and ethos? Three categories emerged: study directed towards the extension of knowledge; the application of knowledge to the solution of projects of direct and immediate benefit to the community; and staff development and the encouragement of creative activities by writers and artists. It is important to note that, unlike the universities, the Polytechnic was not funded to conduct research: it was necessary, therefore, to supply some modest, appropriate resource from its own coffers. Staff were encouraged to seek financial support from external agencies, but they were also given the opportunity to apply for internal pump-priming funds. These bids were scrutinised by validating panels whose criteria included the potential impacts on teaching programmes. Some 163 projects had received assistance by 1975.

The ARCC's work soon bore fruit. Some 100 staff were active in research as early as 1972–3. Most of the activity was in Science and Technology where the research tradition was strongest, but all aspects of the Polytechnic's work were soon involved. Research activity grew slowly but steadily: some 60 staff were registered for higher degrees by 1974; and in the five years 1975–80 grants from bodies like the Science Research Council (SRC) and the Department of Industry (DOI) amounted to some £750,000. Whilst there was growth, the total research output lagged considerably behind that of the typical university. But the Polytechnic was not aspiring to be a typical university, and, since it had not been funded to carry out research, it was content with Chilver's summary of the position: 'while the proportion of total income represented by research grants and contracts is small compared with the two universities, there has been, nonetheless, some growth in recent years'.[14]

The Teaching Company Scheme, which was more concerned with the application of knowledge than its extension, chimed well with the Polytechnic's ethos. Supported jointly by the SRC and the DOI, the scheme aimed to attract more of the most able graduates into careers in manufacturing industry. It placed graduates in industry where they worked on challenging projects under the joint supervision of academics and industrialists. The Polytechnic pioneered the scheme in Northern Ireland. The first Teaching Company, launched in 1978, ran in association with a group of small companies under the aegis of the Northern Ireland Development Agency. The second, a year later, involved Davidson and Company Limited (Sirocco). There were many more to follow.

Consultancy – demonstrating that staff could practise what they preached – complemented research. The Polytechnic Innovation and Resource Centre was established in 1977 to coordinate this work. It promoted the institution's expertise to the community, and facilitated access to that expertise and to an increasing number of resources, including the Centre for the Handicapped, the Northern Ireland Institute of Coaching, the Computer Centre, the Northern Ireland Science & Technology Regional Organisation, the Construction Information Centre, the Regional Teachers' Centre, the Design Research Office, the Polytechnic Education Development Centre, the

14 Chilver's *Final Report*, 87.

Educational Technology Unit, the Social Skills Training Centre, the Industrial Relations Unit, and the Trades Union Resource Centre.

ESPRIT DE CORPS

Ultimately, the Polytechnic's reputation depended on the quality of its staff. The dynamism and potential of the new institution attracted able people who melded with an experienced and committed 'old brigade' to provide a strong corporate thrust and identity. Derek Birley recognised the importance of *esprit de corps* and pride in achievement; and he knew that ownership was the key to success, particularly in an institution that had emerged from an amalgam of different traditions and loyalties. One of the first steps in that direction was the formation of Consultative Committees, initially at Jordanstown, Belfast and Garnerville, to facilitate communication between staff, students and governors on matters affecting social, welfare and recreational development. The Polytechnic's committee structure also helped to involve people. Criticised by some as over-complicated and bureaucratic, it nevertheless provided ample opportunity for people to have their say in the shape and direction of the new venture. The Director was pleased with the results. 'In one sense the achievement of bringing together in purposeful activity so many people from such different places and different standpoints is in itself little short of a miracle'.[15]

Staff numbers grew with the institution. The first staff joined in July 1970 and by February 1974 there were 1,306 in post, 1,029 full-time and 277 part-time. The appointment of new staff and the assimilation of old was a tremendous task carried through by the Establishment Committee, the Establishment Officer and his staff. Professorships were created in 1975. Staff and students were able to enjoy a range of recreational amenities, including sports halls, a swimming pool and squash courts. Intellectual stimulation was provided in plenty in the splendid Library which was a source of pride and a regular stopping-off point for visitors. Completed in 1975, it housed some 167,000 volumes and was able to seat 730 readers. The social side of the Polytechnic began to assert itself. The Polytechnic Club and the Poly Wives Club provided ample opportunities for

15 D.S. Birley, 'The Polytechnic So Far,' 22 February 1974.

wining, dining and gossiping. The newssheet *Polygram*, launched in 1975, did much to improve communications across the whole gamut of activity. The more formal Ulster College Staff Association set up shop in 1975 'to promote the social, recreational and cultural interests of its members and to secure for them facilities and amenities for pursuing such interests'.[16] The rapid growth in staff numbers and the unique nature of the Polytechnic required strong and constructive inputs from the various staff unions.

The students also had their say. Based in Block 11, the Students' Representative Council had six full-time salaried officers responsible for education and welfare, communications, entertainment, and clubs and societies. Student welfare was of crucial importance. Personal problems, poor health, unsatisfactory accommodation and uncertainty about career prospects could impair a student's educational progression. Student Services, housed in its own building, helped students with these problems. A Studies Advisory System provided a link between academic and personal matters. Each student was assigned a member of academic staff as a Studies Advisor who, in addition to assisting with curriculum-related problems, identified and referred personal problems to specialists in Student Services.

A FORCE TO BE RECKONED WITH

The original concept of the Ulster College had revolved around sub-degree work and postgraduate specialisation and had been heavily slanted towards Science and Technology. A mere 2,000 full-time-equivalent students had been envisaged in the long term, but the Polytechnic's rapid development turned Lockwood's predictions on their heads. When the House of Commons Select Committee visited Northern Ireland in 1982, its report on Further and Higher Education pointed out that 'the Lockwood Committee had not been able to predict the rapidity with which the numbers of students and courses would expand at the Ulster College. The growing number of students far outstripped the Committee's 1980–1 projected figures'.[17]

As courses grew in number a need arose for out-centres to bring part-time higher educational opportunities to students outside the

16 *Polygram*, Vol. 1, No. 5 (June/July 1975), 6.   17 *House of Commons, Report on Further and Higher Education in Northern Ireland* (1982), 2nd Report from the Education, Science and Arts Committee, 42.

Polygram

NEWS-SHEET OF THE ULSTER POLYTECHNIC　　　　　**MARCH 1980**

N · SPECIAL EDITION · SPECIAL EDITION · SPE

THE POLYTECHNIC AND YOU

It is a time of decision for sixth-form students throughout the country.

We at the polytechnic are very conscious of the seriousness of such deliberations and it is thus our policy to ~~allow a final decision on whether the~~

23 The *Polygram* newspaper

Belfast area. The Diploma in Management Studies was offered at Londonderry, Bangor and Lurgan, and parts of the in-service BEd ran in the Teachers' Centre at Enniskillen. Formal collaboration extended further afield. In Europe, for example, the University of Caen was a partner in business education, and the Tunku Abdul Rahman College in Kuala Lumpur and Campbell University in North Carolina formed a productive tripartite partnership with the Polytechnic in a range of disciplines. The Polytechnic hosted an increasing number of international conferences, including one in May 1975 on 'The Economic and Business Challenges of Europe', and another, 'Interdesign 76', sponsored by the International Council of Societies of Industrial Design on the theme 'The Designer and the Creation of Employment Opportunities'. Another indicator of the Polytechnic's growing stature was the number of staff invited to participate in the activities of the CNAA and other validating and professional bodies. There were also early successes in the sports arena, with Ulster College winning the women's section of the British Polytechnic Athletics Championships in 1975.

The Polytechnic's increasing effectiveness and status were formally recognised by influential bodies. In 1975 a visiting team of senior inspectors and officials from the DES heaped praise on the Polytechnic's financial systems. In Derek Birley's words, 'the visit helped to transform the College's image in Ulster's corridors of power from an inexplicable, expensive and somewhat undesirable cuckoo in the nest, to a cost-effective and innovatory challenge to existing assumptions'.[18] The reports of the many CNAA visits were, on the

18 D.S. Birley, private communication to the author.

24 The Belfast campus at the time of the merger.

whole, complimentary. The Chilver Report concluded that the Polytechnic clearly constituted a major asset in Northern Ireland's higher education system, and the White Paper which followed described the Polytechnic as a flexible institution with a marked capacity for innovation.

This demonstrable success challenged Lockwood's notion of hierarchies. Envisaged initially as a further education college, the Polytechnic had become a force to be reckoned with. Others were recognising that fact – including those in the corridors of power. In March 1974 the Minister, Basil McIvor, advised the Northern Ireland Assembly of an urgent need to co-ordinate the province's higher education provision. This was to be pursued by an Advisory Committee for the Co-ordination of Higher Education (ACCHE), with membership including the Polytechnic's Director, along with the two Vice-Chancellors (Professor Sir Arthur Vick of QUB and Dr Alan Burges of NUU) and Sir Frederick Dainton, the Chairman of the University Grants Committee (UGC). The Polytechnic was pleased, but wary, about its involvement. In terms of co-ordination, it was confident that it occupied the high moral ground. Every one of its degrees had been submitted to the Department for scrutiny before being launched, and its Council included representation (unreciprocated) from the two universities. But there were fears that this was yet another attempt to clip its wings, and the proposed UGC membership was a matter of particular concern. The Polytechnic asked the Department to ensure that any input from the UGC would be based on knowledge of and sympathy with the aims and needs of the Polytechnic. In the event, for whatever reason, the UGC did not participate. Many meetings were held and there was much intellectual 'arm wrestling', but ACCHE made little advance towards its stated objective of improving the co-ordination of Northern Ireland's higher education provision. Government decided on a harder line and in May 1978 it asked ACCHE to consider the introduction of a new Lockwood-style review of higher education.

IMPENDING APOTHEOSIS

The Polytechnic was not overly enthusiastic about the prospect of yet another in-depth review of its work. Staff were concerned that the process would be a potentially serious distraction from their primary objective of meeting the needs of students and the community. So the Department was informed that Governors would be unlikely to give whole-hearted support to the proposal. However, the review, chaired by Sir Henry Chilver, went ahead, and the Polytechnic, pleased or not, became deeply involved.

The Polytechnic submitted four reports to the Chilver Committee. The major one, over 100 pages in length, offered a frank analysis of the difficulties as well as the achievements of the Polytechnic's early years. It described how it had sought to complement rather than compete with the universities. And, noteworthy in the light of subsequent events, it sought no change in status.

The Government's rejection of Chilver's recommendations came as no surprise to the cognoscenti. But the subsequent proposed merger of the Polytechnic and the New University of Ulster caused much surprise and consternation at Jordanstown. There was concern that the Polytechnic would be emasculated, and a view that energy

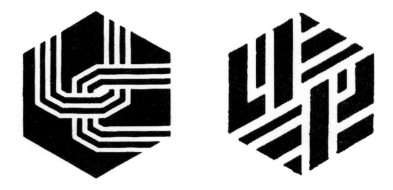

25 Logos: from Ulster College to Ulster Polytechnic.

expended on such an undertaking would be more fruitfully deployed on course development and research. But there was also a realisation that the market place's perception of university status could be used to assist the delivery of the Polytechnic's objectives. At a more personal and practical level there was concern about job security, salaries and pensions.

None of this was helped by the rumoured and real attitudes and comments of the proposed partner, and Polytechnic staff began to grow less enthusiastic about joining forces with such a reluctant ally. But, after much soul searching, the Academic Board eventually agreed to support the merger, subject to what it saw as necessary safeguards. At its meeting on 8 April 1982 the Board welcomed the Government's decision to end the binary system in Northern Ireland and to secure the co-ordination of higher education through two major institutions. It welcomed the notion that these two institutions would be complementary, and that one would embody the particular characteristics on which the Polytechnic's success had been based. And it recommended further exploration of the proposed merger with the New University of Ulster.

So the Academic Board were not to be taken for granted; nor were they going to be rail-roaded. A fairly hot baton was passed to the Polytechnic's representatives on the Steering Group which had been charged with making a reality of the proposed merger.

5

The Merger and After, 1982–1991

ROSALIND PRITCHARD & PETER ROEBUCK

'The merger ... was nothing to do with the interest or the ease of the staff ... to make it worth doing we were obliged to do it the hard way'.[1]

Conceived over two years earlier through a government decision to merge the New University of Ulster and the Ulster Polytechnic, the University of Ulster was born on the day on which its Royal Charter came into operation, 1 October 1984.

Though not the first amalgamation in the history of higher education in the United Kingdom, this was the first attempt to merge two institutions from opposite sides of the binary line – the division between universities and polytechnics. Eight years before the abolition of the binary divide in Britain in 1992, it was primarily the transbinary nature of the merger which made the scheme ambitious and unusually interesting: there was no precedent. There were, however, other issues. Unlike most universities, the University of Ulster had four campuses – at Belfast, Coleraine, Jordanstown and Magee College in Derry – and the distances between them were substantial: 73 miles from Belfast and Jordanstown to Derry; 32 miles from Derry to Coleraine; and 55 miles from Coleraine to Belfast and Jordanstown. Moreover, at the merger there were 11,182 students in the University, a large enrolment by contemporary standards which posed considerable challenges: over half the higher education students in Northern Ireland underwent a fundamental change in their institutional circumstances. Because of these and other complexities of the merger, in 1988 the University Grants Committee described the achievements of the founding period as 'heroic': 'the merger which had, in effect, been a speculative enterprise has proved a great success'.[2] Just four

1 *Vice-Chancellor's Report to the University Court* [hereinafter *Report to Court*], *1988–89*, 18. 2 *Report to Court, 1987–88*, 19.

years after the inception of the new institution, this was a powerful endorsement.

How did the merger come about? What plans were laid for it and how effectively were these implemented? What progress did the University make in its earliest years and how did it engage with the communities which it was established to serve? Above all, what did it feel like to be part of this most radical initiative in higher education in the United Kingdom?

THE WHITE PAPER

As outlined in the previous chapter, Government quickly sidelined Chilver's final Report. On 23 March 1982, having released the Report, it published a White Paper – *Higher Education in Northern Ireland: the Future Structure* – almost simultaneously. This announced that the New University would merge with the Ulster Polytechnic to form a single, multi-campus, university-level institution. The government believed that the existing talents of NUU and of the Polytechnic were complementary, and that a merged institution which combined the stronger features of each of them would be of major benefit to Northern Ireland. It pointed out that the Polytechnic was strong on practical and vocational courses, in which the NUU by comparison was lacking, though its academic standing was good; and that the Polytechnic needed some 'academic consolidation'. It stated that 'the concept of a merger thus provides an opportunity for these distinctive strengths to be combined'. It called for 'fuller use … [to] be made of the Magee campus in meeting the immediate requirements of the Londonderry area'. The anticipated administrative difficulties arising from four locations were acknowledged, but 'separate campuses could be regarded as an opportunity to pursue and achieve a geographical spread of provision, rather than as a burden'. There was stick as well as carrot. Future discussions 'should take place in the knowledge that the only alternative, if they do not reach a successful conclusion, is the closure of NUU'.[3]

Reactions varied enormously. The establishment at NUU responded hesitantly and negatively. Feeling obliged to consult his

---

3 *Higher Education in Northern Ireland: the Future Structure,* HMSO (Belfast, 1982), paras. 3.23, 3.26, 4.2, 4.8.

Senate and to ponder the legal implications of everything he said or did, Vice-Chancellor Cockcroft made only the most cautious statements, maintaining that there was nothing radically wrong with NUU and that the proposed merger was unnecessary. Although later, in NUU's official rebuttal of Chilver, he was much more forthright, he and his senior colleagues seriously underestimated government's determination to see the merger through. Precisely because Chilver's proposals were found wanting, another course had been charted and there was to be no going back. The new structure promised to address three of government's long-standing concerns: the need to co-ordinate higher education provision in Northern Ireland more effectively; over-crowding at Jordanstown; and spare capacity at Coleraine and Magee.

Derek Birley, Rector of the Ulster Polytechnic, faced a difficult decision. He feared that the merger might damage achievements at Jordanstown and Belfast, particularly the Polytechnic's ethos of service to students and the wider community; these should never, in his view, be subordinated to the pursuit of academic prestige. He believed that academic excellence in both teaching and research should be equally valued, and strategically integrated, with a commitment to the service and needs of students and the University's regional, national and international communities. He concluded that such a vision would be best pursued in Northern Ireland by an unequivocal effort to make the merger work. Characteristically, once he had taken his decision, he wanted to get on with it.

Feelings among staff were diverse. At NUU the initial reaction was one of shock coupled with a sense of humiliation, although it was recognised that within a four-campus framework the problem of Magee might be better addressed. While strongly believing in the University, the majority of staff of all grades recognised that its viability was questionable, and that it would go under unless it grasped government's offer. For some, particularly on the academic side, government insistence generated concerns about the status and coherence of the merged institution. A third group saw the White Paper as providing the opportunity of creating precisely the type of university which Northern Ireland required. At the Ulster Polytechnic anxieties focused initially on job security, salaries and pensions. Staff also feared the loss of their institution's distinctive qualities. With considerable justification they were proud of their socially relevant courses, their emphasis on access, the quality of their teaching and the extent of their community outreach. They suspected that these might be lost in the pursuit of a traditional university profile. Yet, while it alarmed some, the prospect of acquiring university status excited others. And so at both institutions there were pro- and anti-merger factions.

The unions/staff organisations involved, notably the Association of University Teachers (AUT), the National Association of Teachers in Further & Higher Education (NATFHE), the Association of Secretarial, Technical & Management Staff (ASTMS) and the Association of Polytechnic Teachers (APT), approached matters constructively. Except for the APT (which did not regard itself as a trades union) all were members of the Irish Congress of Trades Unions (ICTU). In a seminal early development they established a joint trades union merger committee under the auspices of the Northern Ireland Committee of the ICTU which negotiated directly with Swinnerton-Dyer, Chairman of the merger Steering Group. Noticeably, the AUT dealt very effectively with the media after publication of the White Paper. Quickly sensing the importance of developments in Northern Ireland (and their potential for a significant increase in the union's membership), AUT headquarters detailed an official to provide the local Association with special support.

While the tasks confronting the planners were many and varied, the quality of developing personal relationships at every level was vital to their success. For the most part, NUU and Polytechnic staff did not know one another and had undergone very different processes of professional socialization. Now they were to be merged, each had to learn to understand the other's norms and values. After a few months attitudes slowly began to change. Each partner saw characteristics in the other which they could appreciate; the merger might produce a fusion in which the components could transcend their origins and together amount to something more than the sum of their parts. Government's decision began to take root.

THE STEERING GROUP

In June 1982 the Department for Education, Northern Ireland (DENI) established a Steering Group to manage the merger. Its Chairman was Sir Peter Swinnerton-Dyer, Master of St Catherine's College, Cambridge, who had recently chaired the Committee on the Academic Organization of the University of London. His Vice-

26 Nicholas Scott, NI Minister for Education at the time of the merger.

Chairman was Sir Norman Lindop, Director of Hatfield Polytechnic, and a member of the Council for National Academic Awards. Initially there were four other members but provision was also made for a further four, two each representing NUU and the Ulster Polytechnic. Nicholas Scott, the Minister for Education in Northern Ireland, set out broad terms of reference for the Group: 'to be responsible for the planning of the new university institution ... working within whatever financial and other guidelines I ... may give them from time to time, and to report periodically to me'.[4] The Group invited written submissions regarding the new institution: the speed with which it intended to operate was reflected in the early deadline for their receipt – 15 October 1982. Because the University was to begin operations in October 1984, a prospectus had to be issued by March 1983. There was no time to lose.

4 Quoting a letter of 18 June 1982 from DENI to NUU, University Archives, Special Edition of NUU *Bulletin,* 20 July 1982, 7.

Some time was lost, however, in mid-1982 while senior members of NUU wrestled with their responsibilities under their Charter. They wished government to accept their critical analysis of Chilver's final Report and, without this, felt unable to accept full membership of the Steering Group. Permission for Vice-Chancellor Cockcroft to attend as an assessor was refused. Wanting to influence developments without acquiescing in its own destruction, NUU then made nominations to the Group: but two nominees – Sir Peter Froggatt, Vice-Chancellor of Queen's University, and Sir Charles Carter, formerly Vice-Chancellor of Lancaster University – resigned in quick succession. Ultimately NUU's representatives were Professor Palmer Newbould, Pro-Vice-Chancellor, and Professor Bill Wallace, formerly Professor of History at NUU, then at Glasgow University, with the Ulster Polytechnic being represented by Professor Don McCloy, Dean of Technology, and Mr. Michael Murphy, Chief Executive of the Western Education & Library Board in Northern Ireland and a Polytechnic Governor.

There were other complications. In May 1982 the Chairman of NUU's Council, Sir Robert Kidd, requested a two-stage strategy: the first, consideration of the merger's feasibility, and the second, if this requirement were satisfied, the planning process. However, Sir Peter refused to engage in discussion of whether or not there should be a merger, which was beyond his terms of reference. What he did do was to provide firm safeguards concerning the continued employment in the University of existing staff of NUU and the Polytechnic. From the outset this had been a key demand of the trades unions as the basis for a successful merger.

The appointment of a Vice-Chancellor was a further source of difficulty. Having decided that (as with all appointments at this stage) selection was open only to internal applicants, the Steering Group arranged to hold interviews in October 1982. NUU argued for open advertisement in this instance and called for deferment of the appointment, but in vain. Two firm responses ensued. The Steering Group indicated that it would proceed to appoint even if only one candidate emerged, and Nicholas Scott wrote to NUU's Council in terms which are best summarised as 'merge or close'. Derek Birley, the sole candidate attending the selection committee, was appointed Vice-Chancellor designate on 21 October 1982. Bill Cockcroft retired early and was knighted in 1983. From 13 November 1982 Professor Palmer Newbould became Acting Vice-Chancellor of NUU.

27 Professor Palmer Newbould, Acting Vice-Chancellor of NUU, 1982–4.

During the summer of 1983 another crisis was averted, though not without difficulty. For NUU's Charter to be surrendered, its Court had to pass a special resolution by a 75 per cent majority at two meetings a month apart. When the resolution was first put on 27 June, pro-merger votes (at 63 per cent) were insufficient, despite Professor Newbould's strong advocacy of the merger. Government indicated immediately that the establishment of the University would go ahead even without NUU; and that, if a second vote was unfavourable, NUU should not plan for a first-year intake in 1984. A second vote on 21 July produced a 96 per cent majority, which was confirmed by a third (of 98 per cent) on 16 September. In October the Governors of the Ulster Polytechnic also voted to petition the Privy Council for the grant of a new Charter.

Despite these obstructions, the Steering Group lost as little momentum as possible and steadily defined the character of the emerging new institution. A fundamental decision was for a unitary rather than a federal structure: the University would be organised by Faculty, not by campus. Furthermore, it would be managed by a Vice-Chancellor supported by full-time Senior Officers and Deans, normally appointed for four-year terms (not elected). Although the Jarratt Report, advocating professional management of universities, was not published until 1985, ministers anticipated the enormous changes prompted by it, while Derek Birley doubted the efficacy of alternative arrangements. The new institution would be called the University of Ulster; its arms and colours would be those of NUU and its headquarters at Coleraine. As a further symbol of continuity amidst change, its Chancellor would be Lord Grey, then-Chancellor of NUU and formerly the last Governor of Northern Ireland.

The Steering Group quickly devolved academic planning to an Academic Consultative Group, chaired by the Vice-Chancellor designate, which advised on course development, academic organisation, the prospectus for 1984–5, and transitional arrangements for students. In its most imaginative decision, the Group arranged for a Proto-University of Ulster, with formal letter-headings etc., to operate for the year leading to Charter Day. Thereby responsibility passed smoothly and quickly to the new Vice-Chancellor and his colleagues. From this juncture developments gathered momentum.

THE PROTO-UNIVERSITY

Until Charter Day on 1 October 1984 the University of Ulster had no legal existence. Both constituent institutions were obliged to continue to discharge their current responsibilities and to conduct their business separately, expanding everyone's workload. Precedence, however, was given to the operation of the proto-institution. The Academic Consultative Group met finally on 3 October 1983, Proto-Senate first met on 26 October, and Proto-Council in mid-November. Long before then, by the late summer of 1983, all the Pro-Vice-Chancellors, Deans and other Senior Officers had been designated. Appointment of the heads of thirty-seven academic departments followed from the late autumn and during the early months of 1984. A full team was in place by Easter, five months before Charter Day.

28 Knocktarna, the Vice-Chancellor's residence at Coleraine.

Meanwhile, some Senior Officers who were not already based there moved to Coleraine to join Derek Birley, by then living in Knocktarna, the Vice-Chancellor's residence just outside the town.

While urging the incorporation of the strengths and the shedding of the weaknesses of the constituent institutions, government did not seek curtailment of the range of courses. Alongside a breadth of full-time degree programmes, it explicitly encouraged sub-degree and part-time provision, with priority being given to development at Magee. These views chimed well with those charged with establishing the University, who relished the opportunity, particularly at Magee, to formulate courses directed, in terms of both subject matter and level, towards proven successes and areas of potential.

What kind of university was Ulster going to be? The answer was one 'with a difference', the title of a paper laid before the Steering Group by Derek Birley on 14 July 1982.[5] Distinctiveness stemmed largely from the first clause of Article IV of the new Charter: 'the University shall ... advance education through a variety of patterns, levels and modes of study and by a diversity of means by encouraging and developing learning and creativity, for the benefit of the community in Northern Ireland and elsewhere'.[6] Guided by this,

5 A copy of this forty-six page document, which constituted a blueprint for the new institution, is in the University Archives. 6 *University of Ulster: Charter, Statutes, Ordinances and Regulations, 2006–2007*, 4.

principles were established for course development. In vocational and professional areas they should link theory and practice and, in all courses, bridge the gap between 'pure' and 'applied'; emphasise creativity and problem-solving approaches; encourage interdisciplinary and inter-professional perspectives; offer a flexible approach to access; and recognise lifelong needs, including enrichment, professional up-dating and 'second-chance' education. Against this background the University developed an exceptionally broad provision, extending from access courses through Higher National courses, undergraduate and postgraduate taught courses, to post-experience courses and doctoral work. This system of multi-level programmes catered for transfer upwards and downwards, enabling students to locate themselves appropriately according to ability and aspiration. A key early decision was to build this provision systematically. All courses, new and continuing, were subject to formal course planning, evaluation and review procedures, involving external assessors, and explicit follow-up processes for dealing with matters arising.

While these arrangements served the University well, they were initially accorded a mixed reception from those staff unfamiliar with such procedures and jealous of their academic autonomy. Yet, though firm and uniform in some respects, the system adopted was entirely flexible in others. Faculties, for example, were free to decide for themselves who was eligible for membership of their Boards. They also adopted a variety of approaches to the structure of first-year undergraduate studies and the facilitation of delayed and informed choice of final programmes.

Beyond course development, applied research would be undertaken wherever possible, with major emphases on breaking down traditional disciplinary boundaries and stimulating the regional economy. Such research would additionally provide opportunities for community engagement, which was also to be fostered by the expansion of work-based education and by the continuing franchise of appropriate courses to other institutions recognized for this purpose, particularly in the Further Education sector. Finally, the University statutes included an important provision about accountability: the Council was to appoint an independent committee not less than every seven years to examine how well the obligations of the Charter were being discharged.

The courses of the proto-University were marketed energetically. The prospectus for 1984-5 was widely distributed, on time. More significantly, targets for student numbers were exceeded in both 1983 and 1984 – re-assuring and encouraging, particularly at Coleraine and Magee. In terms of student demand, the University of Ulster was immediately successful.

THE POST-MERGER YEARS

While this and much else – for example, the establishment of an effective cross-campus administrative system – was gratifying, and while the pace of development, far from slackening, gathered further momentum, the difficulties arising from the merger were neither easily nor quickly resolved.

In establishing the University Council, the key instrument of governance, the Steering Group sought to embrace a wide range of interests from across Northern Ireland and brought together a diverse body, over forty strong, under the chairmanship of Sir Robert Carswell. The Council provided strong support and assistance with the myriad tasks required to establish the new institution. In its busy and often lively meetings it also challenged the executive as the latter strove, amidst a variety of regional tensions and sensitivities, to implement the merger consensually. Towards the close of the century, in the wake of the Jarratt Report, attitudes towards the size, nature and professionalisation of governing bodies steadily evolved, and in due course significant adjustments were made to the size and role of the Council.

The role of staff and student representatives in the process of merger was generally constructive. Both groups welcomed broader representation in the governance of the new institution than had been available in either NUU or the Ulster Polytechnic. Before long NATFHE and the APT ceased operations at Jordanstown and Belfast, enabling those academic and academic-related staff who wished to do so to join the AUT. ASTMS, of course, already represented staff on all four campuses. Among many staff more positive attitudes towards the merger took time to develop. Underlying fears did not dissipate rapidly and management devoted considerable energy to re-assurance and the bolstering of morale. Some older colleagues in both constituent institutions wished to retire early. Their ability to do so was facilitated by a decision of the University Grants Committee. A premature retirement compensation scheme operated throughout the university sector in 1983–4, but in the case of the University of Ulster it was extended to September 1985. Another consequence was the emergence of promotional opportunities for those in post. Moreover, extending earlier undertakings regarding continuing employment, no staff were required to move to another campus, though later there were a few voluntary re-locations.

Two decisions helped to reassure students. Existing students were allowed to choose their institution of graduation, old or new; and under the new regime, as under the old, no course required attendance on more than one campus. Relations between management and the Students' Union were consolidated by a generous initial financial settlement, welcomed also as a baseline for future negotiations. In view of the merger, and its greatly increased membership, the Union had to devise and establish a new constitution. It did so successfully, also agreeing with the University special protocols for dealing with key features of its business – finance, staffing and premises. While this was a major achievement, one outcome of the University's negotiations with the Students' Union failed to win a consensus among academic staff. At NUU sport had been organised via an Athletics Union, with membership and official posts being open to both staff and students. Henceforward, until recent years, the Students' Union managed student participation in sport and recreation throughout the University of Ulster. However, under the new Sports Union, inaugurated in 2003, joint membership of staff and students was re-introduced with the strong support of both parties.

Especially in the early years, some academics taught on more than one campus; some academic-related and technical staff were also intermittently peripatetic; and Senior Officers and heads of academic and administrative departments saw a great deal of three, if not all four, campuses. For a time communication difficulties were serious, though never quite as intractable as some had envisaged. Various developments alleviated them slowly but steadily. Budgets for travel purposes were extended. A minibus service operated between campuses for staff and student representatives, and for the transport of library and other materials. The University expanded its fleet of vehicles and negotiated favourable hire-car facilities. Though ultimately no option was taken up, Derek Birley even explored the possibility of helicopter transport, a sure indication of how management prized solutions to these difficulties. Nor, initially, was telephone communication easy: until 1985 only eight phone lines were available between Coleraine and Jordanstown. Following negotiations with the authorities, they were increased to 800 overnight, with commensurate arrangements for other campuses. Then, with welcome financial consequences, all cross-campus calls were deemed to be 'internal'. Soon a range of other educational institutions and government offices were included in the University's short-code network. These changes produced dramatic improvements in the conduct of business.

Other electronic systems were actively explored. The latest sound-conferencing equipment was used with increasing effectiveness as participants got to know one another and ceased to feel that they were talking to strangers. Here and elsewhere, burgeoning personal relationships nurtured success. In the mid-1980s the University was among the first institutions to acquire video-conferencing facilities. Outside normal working hours these were successful, for example for postgraduate teaching (as long as there was a staff member at each end of the circuit). However, because early prototypes were exceedingly sound-sensitive, they were subject to interference from building and refurbishment work, and some years passed before satisfactory results were routinely achieved. Other electronic facilities soon came into play. There were debates about which systems to install and some strategic retreats from early mistakes. Staff in Computer Services developed mutually beneficial relations with academics in Computing Sciences, the latter a rapidly expanding group during the later 1980s. The University's physical circumstances strongly encouraged recourse to new technology of all kinds.

Although breakthroughs when they occurred, as with the telephone system, might be dramatic, none of these difficulties was susceptible to quick or easy solution. Their resolution was dependent not merely on closer working relations but on the more optimal deployment of staff across campuses. This was achieved gradually, awaiting the results of staff turnover, further strategic planning, and the successful management of the University's finances to the stage where new appointments were made.

As with all modern universities, funding was a matter of concern, though there were particular institutional reasons for this. At the merger reserves were low: those at NUU had been severely depleted in the period leading up to its dissolution, while under its funding arrangements the Ulster Polytechnic had none. The University's multi-campus nature created diseconomies of scale, and yet refurbishment and physical expansion were badly needed, particularly at Belfast and Magee. Moreover, the activities envisaged for the new institution were not all covered by the norms then utilized by the

University Grants Committee (and later by the Funding Councils). This was especially true of its substantial community outreach activities (a matter which has only been rectified systematically during the past decade). The chief concern, however, was the potential cost of the University's top priority, the development of full provision at Magee. If it was to be successfully achieved, this threatened to be expensive, in terms both of newly-appointed staff and of new buildings and other facilities.

In the event anxiety proved to be misplaced. Capital developments were less problematic than once feared. In 1984–5 the large Orpheus Building, adjacent to the Belfast campus, was acquired. Later, following the successful outcome of a public enquiry, the Magee campus was transformed by the completion of a programme of new building, the first two phases of which were funded by DENI, and a third by the University itself. Recurrent funding also proved adequate, aided by a good deal of cross-campus travel for purposes of teaching, and in general by prudent management: if budgets for items like travel expanded, others had to contract, and there was much belt-tightening. One positive factor for the University's core funding was the favourable treatment of substantial part-time student numbers by government officials for whom they were a novelty in the university sector.

TEACHING

Needing to consolidate developments against a background of financial concerns, Derek Birley was no headlong expansionist and, indeed, particularly at Jordanstown, was not allowed to be by government. Student numbers rose (see Appendix), but only moderately and after intense scrutiny of targets. Nor did growth compromise standards. As some applicants could join sub-degree programmes, the grades required for first degrees were increased, and both they and those achieved rose across the decade; as did staff/student ratios, though only from 11.9 in 1984 to 13.8 in 1990. The overall aim was to maintain numbers in what was already a large university. It was difficult not to do more once Secretary of State Kenneth Baker called for national, 'demand-led' expansion from 1987, especially as Northern Ireland had fewer university places than well-qualified applicants, in contrast to other regions of the UK. Nevertheless, there was no expansion for expansion's sake.

The exception to this approach, agreed with government, was at Magee. In 1982–3 a Parliamentary Select Committee at Westminster, deliberating on third-level provision in the north-west, had recommended the establishment of a Polytechnic there. However, the Derry Civic Committee outlined a programme for the economic regeneration of the city based on higher education courses in a series of vocational areas. This complemented the determination of DENI and the University to implement the structure laid down in the White Paper. The result was what seemed in 1984 an ambitious target of 1,000 students at Magee by the end of the decade which, however, was achieved two years ahead of schedule. Faculties were urged to present fresh, non-duplicatory course proposals for Magee and all did so with commendable speed and imagination. Due to rigorous course planning and evaluation processes, growth was cumulative rather than precipitate, care being taken that numbers did not outstrip resources, including new buildings. Nonetheless, while the campus did not acquire a critical mass until the 1990s, there was sustained growth towards that goal, including annual increases in student numbers, from 1983 onwards.

Government was also intent on improved co-ordination of higher education in Northern Ireland and appointed Sir Clifford Butler to chair a Committee charged with identifying possibly wasteful overlap in research provision between the University and Queen's University, Belfast. The Committee's final Report appeared in December 1987. While dealing with research, the outcome also affected teaching. Recommendations about Physics and Chemistry, with consequent movement of staff from Coleraine to Belfast, were favourable to Queen's, while those about Business Studies favoured Ulster. Others concerning the sharing of Library facilities benefited both parties. Both mounted damage limitation exercises against undue government interference. Derek Birley felt that Butler left a 'not very deep mark'.[7] The University lost some researchers but extended its dominance in an area of immense importance to the Northern Ireland economy.

The decision to pursue painstaking course planning, evaluation and review procedures – the first two normally taking fifteen months to complete – was adhered to firmly. The process anticipated many of the features of the subsequent national system of quality assurance. The Academic Policy Committee scrutinised course objectives,

7 *Report to Court, 1988–89*, 18.

market considerations, content and academic arrangements, while the Development Committee presided over resource issues and student number targets. Each was a Sub-Committee of the Senate and was chaired by a Pro-Vice-Chancellor (Professor Norman Gibson and Dr Harry McGuigan respectively). This adherence constituted a clear commitment to first principles at a time when there was the temptation, and encouragement from government, to seek quick results. Significantly, fitness for purpose was accorded precedence.

Thus, not only were there entirely new courses, there were clear-cut opportunities for reformulating the nature, thrust and content of existing courses, which were pursued persistently, though with varying degrees of alacrity, throughout the University. For example, while more traditional versions of language programmes remained available as major, joint or minor options in Humanities Combined, the main language programmes were entirely new – Applied Languages at Coleraine and International Business Communication (also involving Informatics) at Magee. In addition to the principles laid down for all courses, another issue came into play: the need for complementarity of provision rather than internal competition between campuses. Thus, the Department of History, which operated at Coleraine, Jordanstown and Magee, ensured that its courses did not duplicate one another; and so it had to be with other Departments. Inevitably, some tough decisions were taken: for example, only partly in the light of the Butler Report, a move away from single-subject honours programmes in Physics and Chemistry towards more interdisciplinary and applied science; and the replacement of four-year concurrent programmes with Education by single-subject programmes followed by a one-year Postgraduate Certificate in Education. Other developments were less painful, full of potential and often involved more than one Faculty. There was growing emphasis at Coleraine on Biomedical Sciences and Environmental Sciences. At Jordanstown there was greater integration of the old disciplines of Surveying, Building and Estate Management under the new and more relevant umbrella of the Built Environment. Closer collaboration between Engineers at Jordanstown and Art and Design staff at Belfast generated growth in the area of Industrial Design. These are merely instances of the far-reaching shifts which occurred in the University's provision. There was fundamental and widespread change in what the University had to offer.

Questionnaires were circulated to all students (some 3,200) graduating during 1989, seeking their views on the quality of teaching and other aspects of provision. A 78 per cent response rate revealed that two-thirds rated their experience as 'good' or 'very good'. Staff had to be supported in delivering their teaching to a high standard. The University established a Staff Development Unit to provide training for its large workforce. With the needs of newly-appointed staff primarily in mind, a postgraduate Certificate in University Teaching was launched. Ulster was also among the first universities to establish Distinguished Teaching Awards, which recognised and rewarded excellent teaching.

RESEARCH

Research was one way in which the University made a valuable and strategically important contribution to life in Northern Ireland. Dominated by the public sector, the regional economy's private sector consisted mainly of low technology industry and small and medium-sized firms. While public-sector investment in research and development was comparable with that across the UK, industrially-financed research and development in Northern Ireland was less than half the UK average. Thus, the two universities in Northern Ireland carried much greater responsibility than elsewhere for the provision of research support to industry, commerce, the professions and the community at large.

In discharging this responsibility certain difficulties arising from the University's origins had to be overcome. A research tradition had become well-embedded at NUU: a few staff with very light teaching loads had been primarily researchers, though originally not appointed in that capacity alone. At the Polytechnic research activity was less developed, though not uniformly so. Among some groups, it was at a low level, whereas in others it was developed and successful. The majority of staff there were situated at various intermediate points along this wide spectrum. No-one doubted the need to raise the average level of research activity across the University: but how might this best be achieved and what sort of excellence should the University pursue?

An effective strategy had to be sufficiently flexible to address differing circumstances in dispersed locations. Although the effort was led from the centre by a Pro-Vice-Chancellor, Professor Robert Gavin, research activity flowed through a variety of channels. In some areas, Biomedical Sciences for example, the impetus came from small groups of dedicated specialists; in others, for instance History, the drive was generated by a particular Department; elsewhere through an entire Faculty. The University's response was partly pragmatic and partly systematic. Where activity was vigorous among a significant group of colleagues and within supportive arrangements, it was recognised, encouraged and, essentially, left to grow. Where efforts were successful or at least promising, but nevertheless numerically smaller and more isolated, the University established a framework in which they might thrive. The chosen policy was 'to provide selective support to mission orientated Centres rather than to Departments, thereby attuning ... research more precisely to the market'.[8] Relevance to community needs was a major criterion in the selection of these Centres, which were interdisciplinary in nature and described as such. By 1990 there were eight – Centres for Biomedical Sciences, Energy Research, Health and Social Research, Policy Research, Polymer Composites and the Northern Ireland Bioengineering Centre, the Centre for the Study of Conflict and the Centre for Research on Women. Unlike management's approach to the teaching programme, this policy was not based on hard-earned experience; it was more pragmatic and at times even speculative. Yet, it generated momentum and in the five or six years following the merger many of the Interdisciplinary Research Centres grew as rapidly as the larger and longer-established clusters of activity.

In further pursuit of regional engagement the University sensibly built on legacies. Based at Coleraine, the Industrial Unit drew on University-wide expertise in providing consultancy services for companies in the manufacturing and service sectors and for government departments. There was also fresh growth in the Teaching Company scheme which was a particularly effective way for higher education institutions to contribute to research and development in industry. Under the scheme young graduates (known as industrial associates) or specialist research staff worked with partners on industrial projects over a two-year period. By 1991 there were fifteen teaching companies involving over fifty associates.

---

8 *Report of the Seven-Year Review Committee, 1984–91*, para. 4.5.

While this success was gratifying, it also pointed up a dilemma for both universities. It was not just that small and medium-sized enterprises were dominant in the regional economy: there were relatively few large companies to which researchers could relate. Some staff found it productive to establish partnerships in Britain, mainland Europe and the USA. The private sector, wherever its location, did not yield significant funding. External research income, which rose from a very low level of £0.75m in 1984–5 to £2.9m in 1990–1, was derived overwhelmingly from the public sector – from the European Community and the International Fund for Ireland and, above all, from government departments and agencies. A persistent priority was to expand and diversify external research income.

While there was much work for both universities to do in Northern Ireland, their situation was fundamentally different from that of other UK universities although, for purposes of funding both teaching and research, they were treated identically. This was felt to be particularly inappropriate on the research side in view of the disproportionately important role they played in regional research and development. As a periodic visitor to Northern Ireland and as someone who was also thoroughly familiar with higher education throughout the United Kingdom, Sir Peter Swinnerton-Dyer highlighted this in character-istically colourful fashion in May 1992:

> The two universities are bound to argue (and in our opinion would be right to do so) that it is essential to preserve a viable research base in [Northern Ireland], and that therefore the research components of their grants should be higher than they would be if by some act of necromancy [they] were suddenly translated onto sites somewhere in central England. In an ideal world, this argument might be equally applicable to the support of pure and applied research. But in our judgment, government is most likely to find this argument persuasive in respect of research which has a realistic expectation of enhancing wealth-creation in [Northern Ireland]. Given its background, this must be particularly true for the University of Ulster.[9]

The resolution of this debate, soon to bear fruit in government provision of Northern Ireland Development funding, became more

9 In a letter to Sir Robert Carswell, Chairman of the University Council, *Report of the Seven-Year Review Committee, 1984–91*, ii.

critical as public policy moved towards research selectivity. The University was exempted from participation in the first national Research Assessment Exercise (RAE) of 1986, coming so soon after Charter Day; and was granted limited involvement in the RAE of 1989 where, however, the outcome was more creditable than antici-pated with seven units of assessment getting the average 'three' grade. The RAE of 1992, in which the University was fully involved, saw significant improvement. Ulster was around the middle of the league table, with a number of traditional universities and all the former Polytechnics below it. The secure establishment of a research profile, across if not throughout the University – one of the trickiest tasks of the post-merger years – was on the way to being accomplished.

THE UNIVERSITY AND THE COMMUNITY

If a valuable feature of Chilver's final Report was the recommendation that higher education institutions in Northern Ireland should move closer to their local communities, the University's determination to do so was a matter of principle from the start, stemming from the terms of its Charter. Around the mid-point of his period of office the Vice-Chancellor reflected on what he believed were the University's distinctive features. Along with its system of multi-level programmes, interdisciplinarity, and professional orientation, these included a strong commitment to part-time and continuing education, and community service.

DENI had rightly suggested prior to the merger that, despite associated difficulties, the University's multi-campus nature would bring it closer to more students, and provide it with a keener appreciation of their needs as well as better means of meeting them. Four well-serviced venues rendered part-time study feasible for greater numbers, with some courses being delivered at alternating sites at student request in order to spread travel requirements more equitably. Both constituent institutions had developed successful part-time programmes – NUU largely at postgraduate level and the Polytechnic more substantially and across a broader spectrum – and from 1984 the University had one of the largest part-time enrolments in the sector. At 4,408 in 1990–1, the number of such students exceeded the entire enrolment of some other UK and Irish universities.

Community service was multi-faceted, not least in regard to links with the world of work. The existing portfolio of courses with a substantial work-based element was increased although, in an economy beset by high unemployment, at times this was achieved only with difficulty; not infrequently students pursued their sandwich element outside Northern Ireland. The motivation behind the efforts of the staff in this sphere was the conviction that returning students brought the cutting-edge of practical experience to their final-year studies; some were even offered jobs while on placement, long before graduation. By 1990 a third of full-time courses required students to undertake professional or industrial placement without grant aid but with remuneration from employers. Many other students benefited from shorter, unpaid placements. As a separate qualification following successful completion of major placements, the Diploma in Industrial Studies was extended across the institution. Other groups of students, notably in languages, which required long periods of residence abroad among native speakers, were supported through exchanges organized under the European Community's Erasmus and Comett schemes. The objective of all these endeavours was to produce a skilled workforce, equipped with practical experience.

Particularly via one of the larger Faculties, Business and Management, there was substantial engagement between staff and leaders and middle-managers in business and the professions. In separate initiatives the Faculty established the Small Business Institute and a Centre for Research in Management, and developed a number of MBA programmes. Later, in 1988, to bring clearer focus to management education and in-service training, these elements were consolidated to form the Ulster Business School, which subsequently established a Management Development Centre with an emphasis on executive and company development in marketing, exporting and international business. Anxious to play its part, the Faculty of Humanities launched a Foreign Languages for Exporters service to provide local professionals with language capability in advance of the Single European Market; and, at the request of DENI, organized a Japanese Language Programme for Schools, delivered to hundreds of Northern Ireland's sixth-formers. More generally, the University worked closely with the Industrial Development Board, with the Local Enterprise Development Unit and with the Technology Board to provide scientific and technological advice to government departments. Against a background of continuing violence and political strife, and constrained by limited budgets, none of these endeavours was troublefree: but together they constituted an unremitting effort to see Northern Ireland through to better times.

Major changes were underway in the area of new computer technologies. The University's computer scientists were originally located in the Faculties of Science and of Technology before being formed into an Institute of Informatics in 1986; this was accorded Faculty status in 1991. By then they were making the largest single institutional contribution to the education and training of computer scientists in Ireland. In session 1990–1 government approved, and financed, a major extension at Jordanstown to house them.

Regularly receiving many more applications than it had places to offer, the University devised an effective Schools Liaison Programme. Due to its extensive range of vocational courses, it was also much sought after by those emerging from Northern Ireland's Colleges of Further Education. Relations between the University and the Colleges grew closer. The franchising of courses from the Ulster Polytechnic to Colleges recognised for this purpose had begun on a small scale from 1978 and expanded following the merger, particularly via access courses leading to the award of the Certificate in Foundation Studies for Mature Students. By 1991 some 800 full-time and part-time students were pursuing this second-chance opportunity; Higher National Diplomas began to be similarly franchised. Both were subject to the University's planning, evaluation and review procedures, and laid the basis for further expansion in the 1990s.

Nor should one neglect the University's widespread involvement in the cultural life of Northern Ireland. With staff in Music and Theatre Studies, the Riverside Theatre at Coleraine, a Faculty of Art and Design in Belfast, and a varied array of buildings and grounds, the University presented innumerable public lectures, conferences, exhibitions, concerts and other events: these were enjoyed by staff and students and by large numbers of the general public.

THE ACHIEVEMENT

By 1991 virtually everyone – members of the institution, public representatives, government agencies, the media, and the public – felt that the University had been securely established. Consolidation could now give way to development, though there had already been a good deal of the latter.

It was indeed a University 'with a difference', not just in the particular ways alluded to above, but across the spectrum. In 1990–1 32.4 per cent of its students were part-timers; 16 per cent were enrolled on sub-degree courses; and nearly a quarter of its entrants were over 21 years of age, compared with 15 per cent nationally. And, still rare in the sector at this time, it operated on four campuses, at several outstations and through various other recognised institutions.

In terms of individual contributions, the most sustained and powerful came from the Vice-Chancellor. For Sir Derek Birley, as he became in 1990, the years from 1982 to 1991 witnessed the culmination of a long and distinguished career in education. There were several roots to his success. Sir Derek believed that education was the most valuable asset anyone could acquire: it had to be made as readily available to them as possible. He thought long and deeply about educational objectives and was equally careful in erecting systems whereby they could be attained. Indeed, in plotting ways forward he had a visceral belief in the virtues of continuous planning and analysis. His managerial style was balanced: he was remarkably well-informed about the detail of what was going on, but able nonetheless to leave others to get on with their jobs. He developed a very sound relationship with his paymasters: earning their respect, and dealing with them cordially and on equal terms; but also, as the need arose, very firmly. He had a decidedly strong personality. Once strategy had been deliberated and decided, he brooked no interference – in this sense he always led from the front; and if crossed or thwarted, he was not appeased easily, if at all. Yet, fierce though he could be, he also had the knack of getting on with all levels of staff, together with a noticeably undeveloped sense of status and hierarchy.

He was hugely indebted to those who worked with him. Several colleagues from Jordanstown uprooted homes and families to join the project at Coleraine and Magee; those remaining behind shouldered additional burdens. He equally valued the support of senior NUU staff as critical to the successful implementation of the merger. There were many others who strove wholeheartedly and successfully.

Then there were the hosts of other staff, the 'poor bloody infantry' as they were wont to describe themselves at times of stress, of which there were many. From mid-1983 to mid-1986 four years of normal work was crammed into three, and there was little slackening of pace thereafter. Many were exhilarated by the novelty of the opportunity: all had to work longer and harder than ever before, for steadily diminishing financial returns. Beyond undoubted success, consolation lay in the knowledge that the entire sector, presided over by a government intent on fresh approaches to higher education, was having to learn to live with 'more for less'.

Sir Derek Birley was acutely aware of this. In his considered view 'anyone who was involved in the merger ... or has ever thought about what it entailed knows at least that it was nothing to do with the interest or the ease of the staff. None of us saw it as an end in itself, and to make it worth doing we were obliged to do it the hard way'.[10] It is difficult to disagree with this. Government, wisely, decided on the merger; but its successful implementation was another matter entirely, for which the University staff were responsible. The outcome could easily have been otherwise.

10 *Report to Court, 1988–89*, 18.

6

The Development of the
University, 1991–2006

PETER ROEBUCK

'If [the University of Ulster] loses its reforming zeal then it might as well never have been created'.[1]

A NEW ERA

Sir Derek Birley was proud of what had been achieved in establishing the University quickly and successfully. Yet his valedictory remarks sounded a warning: 'there is good hope that the momentum the University ... has gathered will make it difficult to slow down and impossible to stop, but if it loses its reforming zeal then it might as well never have been created'. He reiterated the point less prosaically in the *Higher Education Quarterly*. The University 'badly needs ... men and women with the scent of reform in their nostrils. Without it UU, for all its very real success and strength, will be vulnerable, especially to reactionary Greeks bearing superficially alluring gifts.'[2] To him the University was far more than the UK's only transbinary merger. It 'would serve the Province but would also make its mark in the wider world'.[3] Its formation signified a start to a new way of doing things in higher education and he urged his successors to seize further opportunities for reform. Paramount was the chance to make

---

1 *Vice-Chancellor's Report to the University Court* [hereinafter *Report to Court*] *1989–90*, 21. In addition to these *Reports*, particularly valuable holdings in the University archives include full sets of the Minutes and Papers of the Council and the Senate, the *Reports* of the Seven-Year Review Committees of 1984–91, 1991–8, and 1998–2005, and the University's responses to various consultation exercises, e.g. its submission to the Dearing Committee.   2 D.S. Birley, 'Crossing Ulster's Other Great Divide', *Higher Education Quarterly*, vol. 45, no. 2 (Spring 1991), 144.   3 *Report to Court, 1984–85*, 18.

universities more responsive to the communities they served and driven by the needs of individual students, full-time *and* part-time.

He was wary of changes underway from the later 1980s and suspected more would come: they might divert the University from its commitments and/or erode its autonomy. Secretary of State Kenneth Baker, had instigated a rapid, market-led expansion of student numbers. Between 1987 and 1992 the UK's undergraduate population grew by 60 per cent. Rising costs dictated a reversal of this policy and from 1993 the admission of full-time home and EU undergraduates was strictly controlled. In 1990–1 came the first revision in the support system since the Robbins Report of 1963. Maintenance grants and parental contributions were frozen and student loans introduced. Then in 1991 all Polytechnics and many Colleges were granted university status overnight. Equally significant were changes in the manner in which this enlarged sector was managed. Since 1919 the University Grants Committee, made up of academics yet disbursing increasing public monies, had constituted a benign buffer between institutions and their paymasters. The Committee's replacement, first by a more representative Funding Council and then by separate Councils for England (including Northern Ireland), Scotland and Wales, inaugurated an era of closer scrutiny of university business. Quinquennial gave way to annual plans. Later separate recurrent and capital grants were replaced by single annual grants (initially subject to 1 per cent 'efficiency' gains), with capital being raised from surpluses of income over expenditure, or externally. Compared with previous arrangements, these changes were radical.

No-one outside Northern Ireland knew the University and the sector better than Sir Peter Swinnerton-Dyer, Chairman of the merger Steering Group and later Chief Executive of the new Universities' Funding Council. In 1992, presenting the *Report* of the University's first Seven-Year Review Committee as its Chairman, he maintained that the period had 'been difficult for even the most securely established universities': 'the next seven years look likely to be even more difficult'.[4] Like Sir Derek, he suspected that things might never be the same again. Nor were they!

4 *Report of the Seven Year Review Committee, 1984–91*, i.

STUDENT RECRUITMENT

In one respect the 1990s were generally unproblematic. Student recruitment, buoyant during the 1980s, remained so. Whereas some British universities struggled for students, in Northern Ireland there were fewer places than qualified applicants. By choice or through necessity, many Northern Ireland students pursued their education elsewhere; a large majority did not return. Meanwhile in 1991 Ulster came fourth among UK universities ranked according to demand and subsequently fell consistently within the top ten. Its on-campus student population grew prodigiously – more than doubling from some 11,000 at the merger to over 24,500 by 2005–6, with most of this increase occurring from 1990–1. The University became the largest in Ireland and among the largest unitary institutions in the UK.[5]

Full-time students increased more rapidly than part-time. While the University remained a major provider of part-time education, that market became increasingly competitive: in particular, from the early 1990s economic recovery made firms, especially the smaller enterprises dominant in Northern Ireland, reluctant to second employees for part-time education. At course level, fastest growth was among full-time undergraduates, whose numbers doubled between 1991–2 and 2005–6. Postgraduate students did not increase as rapidly but growth was impressive, to over 4,000 on taught programmes. By 2005–6 there were almost 700 postgraduate research students, treble the number enrolled at the merger – gratifying given that fluctuations arose primarily through shifts in the availability of grants rather than falling demand. Decline was only in enrolments on sub-degree courses, a special feature of the University which during the 1980s and 1990s both it and government wished to develop. For long this was achieved, within the institution and externally via franchises to the Further Education sector. Later, beyond the millennium, government policy altered, wishing Further Education to acquire this feature of the University's work to establish a clearer boundary between further and higher education. Numbers on sub-degree programmes were reduced, while those undertaking the new four-year Foundation degrees (two years in an Institute/College and two in the University, designed to reduce regional skills shortages) grew rapidly.

5 See Appendix, table 1.

With buoyant demand, quotas for full-time students and financial penalties for non-compliance, recruitment was tricky. Prospective full-time undergraduates applied through UCAS with 'likely' grades, predicted a year in advance of examinations and often markedly different from achieved grades. Applicants could alter their choice of course and university if they wished. Moreover, the cut-off date for quotas was not in late September but at the annual university census in early December, by which time early 'drop-out' had occurred, allowance for which could be made only in the previous August and September. So managing recruitment was like riding a tiger. There were upward fluctuations from approved limits, notably in 1995–6, and subsequent retrenchment. In the early 2000s the University again exceeded quotas and had to rein in recruitment.

In a large and widely-distributed University, campus considerations were important. Much was achieved by careful course planning; by adjustments to Department/School and Faculty structures; and by introducing programmes in new subject areas and re-locating others. Jordanstown, within Greater Belfast, remained the most populous campus, though, particularly from *c*.2000, its growth was more proportionate to capacity than previously. At York Street in the city centre the student body was expanded slowly but steadily, in line with changing views about space and other resources in Art and Design. Coleraine numbers doubled in the decade after the merger and by 2005–6 exceeded 5,500. Magee was transformed. Its expansion had been a key objective, and remained so. By 2005–6 the campus had almost 4,000 students and was scheduled for further significant growth. Many factors contributed to this achievement: physical expansion of the campus, facilitated by Derry City Council; a programme of building and refurbishment; and a commitment by the University to steady, organic growth. Apart from a period of consolidation in 2000–2, there were annual increases in student numbers at Magee throughout the period 1983–4 to 2005–6.

As elsewhere in the UK, the student population was transformed in another respect – gender balance – but not by planning.[6] In 1984 there was a clear majority of males in the University, which subsequently eroded rapidly. Female full-time students exceeded males for the first time in 1986–7, and part-time in 1996–7 – the turning-point in overall totals coming in 1989–90. There was no reversal: by 2005–6

6 See Appendix, table 2.

29 Graduation congratulations from afar?

there were almost 50 per cent more females than males. This came about partly because the elaboration of the University's courses was in subject areas which tended to attract females rather than males. Yet the University enjoyed better-than-average female recruitment in Engineering and Computing Science, which elsewhere tended to attract more males than females. Anecdotally, while Northern Ireland families accepted that sons might travel further afield for higher education, they were less accommodating with daughters. The decisive factor in a competitive market, regionally and nationally, was the ability of women to outperform men in entrance qualifications.

The large majority of students came from Northern Ireland. Those from the Republic of Ireland constituted a substantial sub-group. Their numbers expanded following the ruling in 1986 that EU nationals could study in member countries on the same basis as individuals from host countries; then declined following the abolition of university fees in the Republic in 1996 and the introduction of

30 Graduation Day in Hong Kong.

contributions to fees in the UK in 1997; and ultimately stabilised at 2,000–2,500 students per year. Entrants from Britain, where university places were plentiful, declined dramatically, until they were fewer than overseas students. Thus, students came overwhelmingly from the island of Ireland.

Enrolments were not confined to courses offered on campus. From the later 1980s expansion included students who studied off campus, on courses franchised to institutions recognised for this purpose.[7] There were several strands to this development. The first catered for mature students who had missed out earlier. The University had pioneered this work, the access course inaugurated at Magee in 1973 being the first of its kind. In 1988 the University established an Access Courses Committee which, as part of a national scheme, developed such courses throughout Northern Ireland. By the millennium well over 1,000 students were enrolled annually. Sub-degree programmes, mainly Higher National Diplomas and Certificates, were a second major strand, similarly franchised to other institutions, primarily in

7 See Appendix, table 3.

Northern Ireland. A small number of courses were franchised overseas, in Malaysia, China (especially Hong Kong), and in India and Saudi Arabia. All strands had a common feature: many students completed their programmes, or went on to further study, *within* the University. By 2004–5 there were some 5,123 such students, 1,034 full-time and 4,089 part-time. Finally, the University began to provide qualifications electronically by e-learning: 58 students in 1998–9 grew to 933 by 2004–5.

Thus, by 2005–6 around 30,000 students, not evenly distributed but recruited from all over the world, were enrolled on the University's courses.

MASS HIGHER EDUCATION

Mass higher education was a striking feature of public life from the later 1980s and much debate was devoted to it. In 1990–1, having frozen grants and introduced loans, government encouraged universities to facilitate students by making the academic year more flexible – dividing it into two semesters during which modules were both taught and examined. Under its second Vice-Chancellor, Professor Trevor Smith (1991–9), who strongly supported continuing reform, the University lost no time in implementing these changes. All full-time programmes were taught during two semesters and through semester-long modules by the autumn of 1992, and all part-time programmes a year later. The University went further, inaugurating a period of teaching and assessment during the summer for those who, for any reason, wished to accelerate towards graduation. 838 students were pursuing this option by 1998.

Whereas the objective during the 1980s was cross-campus complementarity between programmes, with any in low demand being discontinued, new undergraduate programmes were developed thereafter, particularly in areas meeting contemporary needs. Examples were in Biomedical Engineering, Biotechnology, Optometry, International Multimedia Design, and Visual Communication, along with programmes combining these and other areas. Previous commitments to planning, evaluation and review were firmly maintained. At postgraduate level, effort was directed towards professional development and career change, with strong growth in taught Diploma/Master's programmes, many of which were part-time. A one-year, full-time Master of Research was instituted; and, influenced by American practice, the University launched a series of taught doctorates.

Under more stringent finances, staff numbers grew slowly, most new posts being directed towards research. It was, therefore, difficult but essential to sustain a reputation for pedagogical innovation. High student contact hours had been valued in the Polytechnic. These were eroded and, as in other universities, effort was directed to ensuring that teaching and assessment methods catered appropriately for growing student numbers. No ready-made solutions existed. In addition to establishing a postgraduate Certificate in University Teaching (eventually made compulsory for all newly-appointed and otherwise unqualified staff) and inaugurating Distinguished Teaching Awards, additional resources were channelled into staff development, particularly for the teaching role. From 1994 an Educational Development Unit worked with the Staff Development Unit, stimulating pedagogical innovation, promoting good practice and disseminating skills for independent learning. The University participated in various national initiatives, for example those concerned with Enterprise in Higher Education and Tutoring in Schools. The latter scheme, with students mentoring pupils in primary, secondary and special schools, became the most highly developed in the UK. Yet it was surpassed by work-based learning, backed for successful students by the award of the Diploma in Industrial Studies, as a means of equipping vocational courses with a cutting edge. By the mid-1990s a large number of full-time undergraduates undertook work placements integral to their courses, salaried, and of one year's duration in Northern Ireland, Britain, the Republic or overseas. These endeavours reflected Vice-Chancellor Smith's conviction that the University should 'seek to be "of our time" and take our direction from its needs'.[8]

Growth prompted adjustments to internal structures. For a decade after the merger the University worked through 37 Academic Departments located in 8 Faculties; from 1994 these Departments became 20 Schools. Many administrative functions were rationalised, some being overseen henceforward by professionally qualified Directors instead of Pro-Vice-Chancellors – Physical Resources and Educational Services; and later, Human Resources and Corporate Services. Faculties and Administrative Departments assumed greater

8 *Report to Court, 1991–91*, 16.

responsibility for their own affairs: in Professor Smith's view, 'a large, complex and geographically dispersed organisation … cannot be effectively operated by tight central control over all its multifarious activities'.[9]

After years of pre-occupation with the merger the University had perhaps become somewhat introspective. Further initiatives sought to ensure that it punched its weight. Links with the community were strengthened by the appointment of over forty Visiting Professors by 1995. New posts were established – International Officer, Alumni Officer, and Director of Development, all within a new Pro-Vice-Chancellorial portfolio of External Affairs. In 1993, in a joint project at Magee with the United Nations University, an International Centre for Conflict Research (INCORE) was founded to elaborate the earlier, seminal work of the University's Centre for the Study of Conflict.

RESEARCH

As we have seen, the new, national approach to university management included periodic assessment of research to promote excellence and secure value for money. Hectic growth, with consequently increased costs (but not commensurate funding) brought research performance under close scrutiny, with broadly positive results. It was increasingly appreciated that Northern Ireland's two universities were not only major educators. Compared with institutions elsewhere, they also contributed substantially to research and development, a crucial role in a regional economy with a weak private sector and where the universities themselves were among the very largest employers.

Recognising, along with most other universities, that it could not achieve excellence in all areas of research, the University pursued a policy of selectivity, directing resources to areas of strength and potential, and establishing interdisciplinary research centres. In the Research Assessment Exercise (RAE) of 1992 the University significantly improved on its performance in 1989. Moreover, government heeded advice about the strategic value of research conducted in both universities, and Northern Ireland Development funds were provided on a competitive basis. In 1993 the University established a Research Office, subsequently an increasingly effective hub for co-ordination

9 *Report to Court, 1993–94*, 2.

and further development. All bore fruit in the 1996 RAE when strong
headway was recorded in all major criteria: the number (369.5 in 1992,
495 in 1996) of research active staff and their output; research students
(392 in 1992, 596 in 1996); and external funding (considerably more
than for any post-1992 universities).

Engagement with industry, especially in Northern Ireland, gathered
momentum. Several Applied Research Centres were established, either
within the University or with partners. The University became 'the
leading UK practitioner'[10] in the national Teaching Company
Scheme, whereby it and businesses collaborated on company-specific
projects, using innovators some of whom became available for
subsequent recruitment. UUTech Ltd, formed in 1998, assumed
responsibility for technology transfer, exploiting potential scientific
applications through patenting and licensing, and creating incubator
units for spin-out companies. The University laid careful plans to
establish Science Park activity. Support for advanced industry and the
attraction of inward investment to Northern Ireland both depended
on a first-class research base. It was also important to place new
businesses adjacent to the best researchers, so the Science Park was
distributed across three sites with differing specialities – bioscience at
Coleraine, technology for business at Jordanstown, and software
development at Magee.

DEARING AND AFTER

Diversification did not erode distinctiveness. With four campuses and
various outstations in a region emerging from civil strife, the
University's situation was unique. It accorded parity of esteem to
vocational and non-vocational courses; adjudicated even-handedly
between different entrance qualifications, including GNVQs; was
committed to linking theory and practice; and enjoyed productive
relations with numerous public bodies. Key features differentiated it
from others. In addition to numerous mature entrants, part-timers,
and those enrolled on sub-degrees, over half of its students came from
families in social-class categories iii–v (compared with 37 per cent for
the UK as a whole). In terms of widening participation, the
University was, and remained, ahead of its peers.

---

10 *Report of the Seven Year Review Committee, 1991–98*, 69.

What Ulster shared with other universities was anxiety about shrinking funding. By the mid-1990s there was a consensus that the sector faced a funding crisis. The amount that universities had to spend on teaching had halved and funding for infrastructure and research had fallen substantially. Lord Dearing led a National Committee of Inquiry into Higher Education, which reported extensively in the summer of 1997. Its chief recommendation – that students make a means-tested contribution to the fees charged for courses – was accepted, but (departing from Dearing) the government also abolished maintenance grants. Additionally, the University was disappointed by the neglect of Dearing's recommendations relating to Northern Ireland, which sought to create regionally-specific arrangements for co-ordinating and financing tertiary education in the Province. There was equal concern about how local students would fare under the new funding regime.

Changes in the student support system in 1990–1 had already produced alterations in student life. The University was among the first systematically to canvass the views of successive graduating classes and by 1996 over half the respondents replied that they had felt obliged to undertake term-time employment while undergraduates. Student numbers continued to rise after Dearing, but so too did term-time employment. By 2004 Northern Ireland was the lowest region in the UK in the percentage of students receiving financial support from parents (35 per cent against the national average of 51 per cent); and the highest in students needing part-time work to support their studies (61 per cent against 39 per cent). The profile of so-called full-time students changed rapidly in response to the deterioration in their finances. Students became more demanding as customers, seeking value for money, and the University invested heavily in the facilities supporting their work.

FRESH DEPARTURES

Graduate surveys demonstrated that the use of information technology was burgeoning. Mutually reinforcing factors enabled the University to gain a high reputation here. Management quickly identified the need to replace centralised facilities with a more dispersed system, and in 1989 launched a programme for providing microcomputer laboratories across the University. Academically,

31 The Learning Resource Centre at Magee.

Informatics had gained Faculty status and before long employed the largest group of computer scientists in the UK. The Northern Ireland government played its part, facilitating in 1994 the linkage of both universities to an Information Superhighway via JANET, whereby networks were greatly enhanced. Several funding bids were successful for projects exploiting these developments for teaching and learning; and in 1998–9 the University became the Funding Councils' Computers in Teaching Centre. In 2004–5 it was chosen, along with Loughborough University, as the Higher Education Academy's Subject Centre for Information and Computer Sciences.

The new technology prompted other changes. With funding provided following the Follett Report of 1994, the Library came to rely increasingly on electronic communications. A decade later, for example, it was possible to access, in full text, on and off campus, some 14,000 journals. Similar processes came to dominate the distribution of management information and administrative procedures generally, not least those involving students. The University won plaudits for its website and the bulk of its activities, internal and external, came to be conducted electronically. In a fundamental restructuring in 1999–2000, Information Services became still more focused on students, each of whom, full-time and part-time, gained direct access to e-mail and other facilities. The University went on to build state-of-the-art Learning Resource Centres at Jordanstown and Magee, where Library and Computing Services came together; similar facilities were later provided at Coleraine and Belfast. Students used the Centres heavily from the start.

These Centres were part of an extensive building and refurbishment programme which, in less than two decades, transformed the University's premises. The Funding Council commissioned a sector-wide condition survey in 1992 which revealed a massive requirement for backlog maintenance. The University had anticipated the professional property management system which this situation demanded and from the early 1990s established separate budgets for major capital works, minor works, and maintenance, whose deployment was integrated with corporate strategy and, more specifically, with academic and operational plans. Apart from the splendid neo-Gothic main building at Magee, and the former Professors' houses in College Avenue created from the late nineteenth century, the bulk of the University's premises dated from the late 1960s and early 1970s. Because most buildings were relatively young, it had been assumed (mistakenly, but as elsewhere in the sector) that they needed little maintenance. With generous support from the Northern Ireland government, newly-instituted programmes steadily rectified this. Fifteen or so years later over half of UU's premises were in the Funding Council's top two categories of fitness for purpose. Appropriately in a University with a major commitment to environmental science, this achievement was complemented by an energy policy. The University surpassed the targets for reducing energy consumption set for it by government, despite growing student numbers and major, additional building complexes.

32 The Centre for Rehabilitation Sciences at Jordanstown.

33 The Centre for Marine and Coastal Science at Coleraine.

The estate was also rationalised and expanded. The addition of Aberfoyle (a mid-nineteenth century industrial magnate's house) in 1998 and the Foyle Arts Centre (a splendid Georgian building of 1814) in 2003 doubled the acreage at Magee; the former Northern Ireland Hotel and Catering College at Portrush was integrated with the Coleraine campus in 2002; and 50 acres of land abutting Jordanstown were acquired in 2004. Meanwhile, the University exited from leased premises at Jordanstown, and at Carrickfergus where the work of the Technology Unit was moved back to the Jordanstown campus; and it sold the former Freshwater Biology facility by Lough Neagh. Inevitably, however, it was the new building programme which commanded most attention.

Although underway earlier, this programme was driven forward most energetically by Professor Gerry McKenna, third Vice-Chancellor (1999–2004). The new facilities consisted primarily of specialist research space – the Harry Ferguson Village and the Centre for Rehabilitation Science at Jordanstown, the Centres for Molecular Biosciences and Marine and Coastal Research at Coleraine, and two Research Pavilions and the Technology Software Innovation Centre at Magee. These campuses also saw major development of the Science Park sites. Yet the programme was not confined to research facilities. In addition to the Learning Resource Centres and the creation of major, refurbished public spaces, there were two new crèches; imposing headquarters at Jordanstown for the Northern Ireland Sports Institute; and at Coleraine, Jordanstown and Magee, both on and off campus, extensive, high-quality student accommodation. Development capital came from new sector-wide funding opportunities; the Northern Ireland government; major donations (particularly from Atlantic Philanthropies, to whom the University was hugely indebted); and savings, though in the case of student residences none was required. Beginning with the tax-efficient Business Expansion Scheme of the early 1990s, the provision of student accommodation was via a succession of public/private partnerships, with entrepreneurs raising the capital, thereby enabling the University to reserve its own capital for other projects. The building programme continued, with the latest project – the replacement of buildings on the Belfast campus – being the longest-awaited and most ambitious of all. During a period when University staff nationwide sustained significant real-terms reductions in salaries

34 The Harry Ferguson Engineering Village at Jordanstown.

and wages while dealing with a rapidly growing student population, building and refurbishment at Ulster provided them, and their students, with greatly enhanced working facilities.

Other changes – originating from government and internally – had a beneficial effect on individual members of the University. As elsewhere, considerable resources were devoted to discharging legislative responsibilities, some of which, e.g. concerning Fair Employment, were designed to rectify past problems in Northern Ireland. Section 75 of the *Northern Ireland Act 1998* required designated public authorities (of which the University was one) to promote equality of opportunity and good relations between persons of different religious belief, political opinion or racial group. The University's equality scheme had to outline the action it would take to comply with the legislation and, for the future, all new policies were screened to eliminate possible adverse impacts. A *Disability Discrimination Act* was gradually phased in, a key juncture occurring in 2005 when the Special Educational Needs and Disability Order came into force. Under this, staff, when confronted with demonstrable need, had to make reasonable adjustments to learning facilities, including the services associated with them. Across the period Health and Safety legislation was passed, requiring not only heavy expenditure but also the creation of more effective procedures, including consultative groups at University, Faculty/Departmental and campus levels. A rolling series of safety audits was introduced, as were new sickness, absence and stress management procedures.

Paying more for their education and working part-time to make ends meet, students required improved institutional support. The student complaints system was strengthened. Examinations (and where practicable coursework) were marked anonymously. Student Welfare services diversified: a dedicated team, operating on all campuses, provided health, childcare, guidance and counselling, disability and financial services, with rights and responsibilities laid out in a Support Charter. Staff were also the subject of similar new departures. The University revised its policy regarding bullying and harassment; and further elaborated its family friendly policy in terms of maternity/paternity leave and pay, and leave for purposes of adoption, the care of dependants, and following bereavement. While growing rapidly, the University acted in support of individual students and staff.

CORE BUSINESS

Amidst continuous change it was essential that the University's structures were fit for the discharge of core business – teaching and learning, research and knowledge transfer, and the facilities to support them. At the millennium, with this in mind, Professor McKenna embarked on further re-structuring of Faculties, Schools and Administrative Departments. A key decision was to develop major but complementary strengths through consolidating campus-specific disciplines; and to design linked or interdisciplinary programmes from the available subject mix. The Faculty of Life and Health Sciences was further concentrated at Coleraine (along with the School of Hotel, Leisure and Tourism at Portrush). Moving from Jordanstown

35 A research pavilion at Magee.

and Coleraine respectively, Music and Theatre Studies contributed to
a major concentration of Performing Arts at Magee. Following similar
moves, Social Work and Social Policy were also centred at Magee.
Subsequently, via the modular system, there was strong growth in
combined and interdisciplinary programmes which offered employment
opportunities and met market demand in terms of student preferences.
The University's statutes were also amended to allow joint awards,
thereby further promoting fruitful partnerships. By 2003–4 nearly 600
individual undergraduate programmes were available; and, against the
national trend, recruitment remained strong with, for example, some
38,000 applications for entry in 2005.

    The potential of e-learning was exploited, both to compensate for
downturns in traditional markets for part-time courses and to support
a diverse student population. In 2000 an Institute of Lifelong
Learning was established with a remit to embed e-learning throughout
the institution. A year later *Campus One* – the vehicle through which
all the University's e-learning programmes were delivered – was

launched. By mid-decade one-third of all part-time postgraduates were studying online and enrolments included students from 45 countries. The University's e-learning portfolio was the largest in the UK, enhancing its reputation as an innovator. While students were attracted from overseas, a large proportion of the demand came from closer to home. During Semester 1 2005–6 some 19 per cent of distance learners were from Northern Ireland, 33 per cent from the rest of the UK, 35 per cent from the Republic of Ireland, and 13 per cent from overseas.

Students on campus also benefited, particularly from access to WebCT, the University's virtual learning environment. By 2004–5, when some 16,000 of them were using the system, over 1300 active modules were on offer, with others in preparation. Deemed a 'lighthouse institution'[11] in this regard, UU was subsequently one of only two universities in the UK to be recognised by the InniUniLearning project, funded by the European Commission to foster innovative e-learning strategies in higher education.

Another fundamental development was the external assessment of the quality of teaching and learning. In 1990 the Committee of Vice-Chancellors and Principals, acknowledging the need for independent assessment of universities' quality assurance mechanisms, set up the Academic Audit Unit. Audits examined how an institution pursued its aims and objectives against the codes and guidelines for good practice already published by the Committee. This approach proved too flaccid for government who, through the *Further and Higher Education Act, 1992*, established the Higher Educational Quality Council, which conducted much tougher audits. The Funding Councils also embarked on a long series of quality assessments, subject by subject. Then in 1997, in the wake of the Dearing Report, both audits and subject-based assessments were taken over by the Quality Assurance Agency for Higher Education (QAA).

Amidst these and other developments universities soon voiced bitter complaints about erosion of their autonomy, and UU was no exception. University life was 'punctuated with a series of seemingly endless demands to compile further information and to receive visitations of inspectors probing into corporate governance, teaching assessment, quality audit, estate management, employment policies and so on'.[12] The peregrinations of the QAA were judged to be unduly onerous and in

11 *Report to Court, 2001–02*, 13–14. 12 *Report to Court, 1994–95*, 3.

36 The Centre for Molecular Biosciences at Coleraine by night.

2001–2 a sector-wide clamour for a lighter touch finally prevailed. The new process incorporated elements of subject-level enquiry within each institutional audit visit. Assessors still called at regular intervals, but there were fewer of them and their visits were less frequent.

In the period 1990–2006 the University participated in thirty-four subject reviews, two audits of collaborative provision and one of overseas provision, and three institutional audits. Outcomes were favourable. Indeed, the institutional audit of April 2005 provided a ringing endorsement of UU's endeavours to provide high quality education. The QAA highlighted five features of good practice: a commitment to, and achievement of, an embedded academic quality culture; a systematic approach to strategic University developments; the effectiveness of staff development activity; a coherent and comprehensive strategy in regard to e-learning; and the comprehensive provision for the support, training and supervision of research students.

In research and knowledge and technology transfer, activity intensified following the encouraging performance in the Research Assessment Exercise (RAE) of 1996. A fresh research strategy was launched in 1997. Under this management became more explicit through Coordinator-led Units of Assessment which were funded directly by RAE-derived Quality Research (QR) monies, portions of which were retained centrally for strategic investment in areas of strength or potential. This more focused approach produced an enhanced performance in the RAE of 2001, with upward shifts both in ratings and the number of staff contributing to them. Highlights were the retention of the 5* (the highest rating) won by Biomedical Sciences in 1996 and the award of a 5* in Celtic Studies (Irish); and grades of 5 in Art and Design, the Built Environment, and Law. In preparation for the RAE of 2008, 17 Research Institutes (some comprising several Units of Assessment) provided an even closer focus of resources on the most successful researchers, ensuring that institutional arrangements were tightly geared to the promotion of excellence.

All this was paralleled by growth in the University's research facilities and capacity. At £6.7M in 1997–98, research income derived directly from government doubled to £13.5M by 2005–6. Across the same period additional income, from grants and contracts, trebled; and, exceptionally in 2000–1 and 2002–3 totalled £36.2M and £33.9M respectively. Much of this funding came through success in competitive national and regional exercises. Examples of major developments funded in this way were the Fire Safety Engineering Centre at Jordanstown, the Centre for Molecular Biosciences at Coleraine, the Academy for Irish Cultural Heritages at Magee, and the Centre for Research in Art, Technologies and Design at the Belfast campus; but there were several others, some involving new building, some new staff, and some both.

Following earlier success, the University was an acknowledged leader in Knowledge Transfer Partnerships (as the Teaching Company Scheme was now known) and in Fusion (its cross-border equivalent). It worked closely with development agencies, particularly Invest Northern Ireland, and was singled out for praise in the Treasury's Lambert Review of 2003 as 'demonstrating excellence in driving forward regional economic regeneration'.[13] One major new scheme established Research, Training and Development Centres of Excellence, of which four were sited in the University – in Functional Genomics, Software Processing Technologies, Company Incubation for Engineering, and Intelligent Systems. All were in areas where the research base was thought likely to prompt development of intellectual property that

13 *Report to Court, 2002–03*, 32–3.

37 The Technology and Innovation Centre at Jordanstown.

might generate new knowledge-led businesses or reinforce existing ones. Another important initiative, in which the University participated energetically, was Invest Northern Ireland's Proof of Concept scheme, which provided funding to investigate whether particular pieces of intellectual property might lead to new products or services.

UUTech Limited undertook a comprehensive review of its operations in 2004–5. It managed knowledge and technology transfer activities, from technology disclosure through to licensing and/or spin-out; it assumed the commercial leadership of Proof of Concept projects awarded by Invest Northern Ireland; and its remit also included the development of consultancy activities. The Science Park sites were the responsibility of another company wholly-owned by the University, UUSRP Limited. At Coleraine, by now, work was largely devoted to the Life, Health and Environmental Sciences. The main focus at Jordanstown was on advanced engineering and medical devices; and at Magee on software development and advanced IT. In 2005 UUSRP supported 25 companies that employed over 350 staff.

CHALLENGES AND DIFFICULTIES

The 1990s therefore, witnessed unprecedented change and development with a very substantial expansion of the student body, many of whose members had working lives quite different from those of their predecessors twenty years earlier. While a great deal was achieved, there were significant challenges and difficulties, not all of which were overcome easily or successfully.

Government policy, operating both through the Quality Assessment of Teaching and the Research Assessment Exercise, unwittingly promoted an uncreative tension between the duties and responsibilities of university staff as teachers, their output as researchers, and their contribution to the community in a variety of other ways. Increasingly, talented and productive all-rounders became an endangered species. Few, if any, institutions resolved this dilemma.

In UU's case other problems arose because of external developments over which the University had no control. During the 1990s, for example, collaboration with the Further Education sector proceeded less smoothly than it might otherwise have done due to the understandable pre-occupation of the Colleges with their own incorporation. Thereafter the sector was subject to a lengthy review, instigated in 2001 by a Northern Ireland Assembly Committee. In September 2005 the government announced that the sixteen Institutes/Colleges would re-form into six area-based institutions. This was implemented during the following two years, though the broader impact has yet to emerge. In the interim, government embarked on a review of the public administration of Northern Ireland in order to reduce public expenditure to levels more commensurate with those elsewhere in the UK. The wide-ranging results of this exercise – potentially generating an annual saving of £200m – affected local government, education, and health and social services (and, therefore, many of the University's partnerships). This review might reasonably be described as the biggest potential rationalisation in the public sector in Northern Ireland since the University was granted its charter in 1984 and, indeed, since the Macrory reforms of 1973. How, and to what extent, the configuration will be altered following political devolution remains to be seen.

Thus, UU conducted its business against a shifting background. Some would argue that it expanded too rapidly. While the University remained committed to being unitary rather than federal, hectic growth across four dispersed campuses exacerbated the problems of communication, internal and external, to be found in any large institution with numerous partners and community links. At times staff felt unconsulted and far removed from decision-making; not infrequently, partners were confused by change within the University and, consequently, sceptical of its efficacy. Yet, had the University not enjoyed a presence across Northern Ireland, it would have been more remote from many of its clients and customers, and its objectives would have been pursued less effectively.

One consequence of growth was mundane but nonetheless controversial – the need for the University to introduce a car-parking scheme in 2004 as a means of managing access to its campuses. This generated widespread criticism, internally and externally, not least because charges were initially set at too high a level. One of the first tasks of the fourth Vice-Chancellor, Professor Richard Barnett (2004–), was to revise the scheme to the point where, while remaining viable, it commanded broad acceptance. In the modern world an institution large enough to be a community in its own right, yet embedded within an even larger community, had to remain sensitive to the views of both.

There were other challenges. It was agreed by government and both institutions that the Northern Ireland Hotel and Catering College at Portrush should integrate with the University from 1 August 2002. A number of highly cognate disciplines – Human Nutrition, Food Technology Management, and Retail Services Management – had been developed at Coleraine and the University sought to establish a centre of excellence in the newly-established School of Leisure, Tourism and Hospitality Management at Portrush. Recruitment, however, was sluggish and the hotel industry in Greater Belfast was persistently critical of its geographical location. Hospitality Management re-located to the new-build campus at York Street, with other staff from Portrush transferring to Coleraine. In pursuit of further expansion at Magee, the University also became engaged in public debate about the feasibility of establishing a North/South Medical School in the North-West. No decision was taken: but seeds were sown.

Among the seeds which conspicuously failed to germinate were the plans laid throughout much of the 1990s to develop a campus at Springvale in West Belfast. Such a development, it was hoped, would make a strategic contribution to widening participation and economic regeneration in a part of Northern Ireland where educational attainment and rates of employment had long been unacceptably low. Initially the campus was designed to be exclusively part of the University; later the proposal was altered to include the Belfast Institute of Further and Higher Education. At the turn of the decade, however, despite the attraction of some external funding, the University became less and less convinced that the venture was financially viable, not least because of the proposed split of student numbers between the two institutions; though it was a condition of government support that it be financially self-supporting. Within both government and the University there was opposition to the notion of moving activities from the long-established York Street campus. Nor was broader political and public support for the project widespread. The decisive factor was financial. In September 2002 the University withdrew from the scheme: ultimately it attracted criticism for its handling of the matter but not for its decision.

Another area where the University's efforts were unavailing was in regard to student finance. Throughout this period, concern grew about the underfunding of higher education. The emergence of knowledge-based economies abroad sharpened anxiety about the effects of persistent underinvestment in this sphere. Government policy emerged in January 2003 in a White Paper, *The Future of Higher Education*. This led to the *Higher Education Act* of July 2004, which catered for the introduction in England of variable 'top-up' fees of up to £3,000 a year with effect from session 2006–7, adopted in Northern Ireland as the *Higher Education (Northern Ireland) Order* of 6 April 2005. Ulster was one of the few UK universities to campaign vigorously against this policy, conscious of the serious implications for social inclusion. In 2004, for example, nearly 40 per cent of its full-time, first degree entrants were from traditionally socially excluded backgrounds, against the national average of 29 per cent. The University's response was to devote one-third of the income from this new source (a sum of £2.2m) to the provision of non-repayable bursaries for students from households with low incomes. It also set aside £300,000 to boost outreach activities aimed at promoting widening participation. Along with everyone else, it awaited with some trepidation the outcome and further development of this radical change in the financing of higher education.

38 The Jordanstown campus, 2004–5.

A THIRD STRAND OF FUNDING

In regard to other seminal matters there were grounds for satisfaction. As the funding crisis deepened in the late 1980s and 1990s anxiety was fuelled not just by severe reductions in support for teaching and the decay of research infrastructure. Universities engaged in other activities for which little or no funding was provided. This had been highlighted by Sir Derek Birley in 1985 in his first report to the University Court. The Secretaries of State for Education and Science in Scotland, Wales and Northern Ireland had published a Green Paper in which they argued that it was 'vital for our higher education to contribute more effectively to the improvement of the performance of the economy'. They went on to recommend practical measures whereby universities might achieve this: 'industrial contracts, consultancy, appointment of businessmen to governing bodies, joint academic appointments with businesses and other employers … the appointment of industrial liaison officers … teaching companies, business clubs and industrial professorships'. Sir Derek's retort, which subsequent developments reinforced, was that Ulster 'emerges as a progressive example of what is sought [because] all of these already have their place in the University'. However, 'to what extent these aspects of our work may result in enhanced future financial support remains to be seen'.[14]

Some of the 93 recommendations in Dearing's massive report – one luckless reader wound up 'in Casualty with a broken foot when he dropped it!'[15] – advocated a stronger regional and community role for universities, and funding to support it. This began to become available from 1999 via the Higher Education Reach Out to Business and the Community (HEROBAC) scheme, and was followed by further initiatives. The universities in Northern Ireland gained access to pockets of funding for particular purposes, though income from this source did not keep pace with developments in Britain. This imbalance was steadily rectified, complementing the high priority which the University had always accorded to its regional role. This role was a primary motivation behind Science Park activity and the strong growth of research facilities and organisation in the years surrounding the millennium. Nor was it confined to those areas. Under a Strategy for Cultural Development, adopted in 2003, there was growing collaboration with the creative industries in Northern Ireland, particularly via the Arts Council. The Faculty of Business and Management contributed significantly to the economy via advice and training for organisations in both the private and the public sectors. On another front, partnerships with local Councils were strengthened and broadened.

One particular initiative proved outstandingly successful, clearly reflecting the University's commitment to widening participation and engagement with the community in pursuit of it. *Step-Up* was an innovative, interventionist programme which sought to provide new learning opportunities in science for young people living in areas of economic and social disadvantage and with a history of low participation in higher education. The programme aimed to raise school pupils' academic performance and their aspirations, thereby enabling them, if they so wished, to progress to higher education. In 2000 *Step-Up* commenced operations in selected schools in the Derry area, chosen according to criteria which, for example, included the percentage take-up among pupils of free school meals. Delivery was via a partnership between the University and schools, local industry,

14 *Report to Court, 1984–85*, 21–2. 15 *Education Guardian*, 24 July 2007, 1.

hospitals and government agencies. These organisations combined in teaching the Advanced Vocational Certificate in Education within a highly-structured programme of academic and vocational activities. Completion and success rates were very high and, with many of them initially having little or no inclination to do so, around 96 per cent of participants progressed either to the University of Ulster or to other universities, frequently to high-demand programmes. *Step-Up* received numerous accolades and, with the help of £1.6m of funding from the Renewing Communities Action Plan and the Department for Employment and Learning in Northern Ireland, the programme was extended to selected schools in the Belfast area from 2006–7. As a premier flagship scheme, *Step-Up* drew further attention to the University's success in widening access. In this sphere it was now widely acknowledged as a leader.

THE FUTURE

Key aspects of continuing development were organisational changes designed to render the governance of the University more effective. This, too, had been a major theme of the Dearing Report; and the University's second Seven-Year Review, published two years later in 1999, was much pre-occupied with it. Not surprisingly, given the origins of the University, its Council was originally largely representative in nature, with a membership of 43. This was reduced to 30 in 2000. There followed in succeeding years a thoroughgoing review of the committee structure of the Council, and the adoption of a statement of primary responsibilities and a framework of delegated authority. The subject of widespread consultation, the Corporate Plan dealing with the period 2006–7 to 2010–11 committed the institution to the provision of excellent learning opportunities; the pursuit of first-class research in selected areas; the maintenance of previous success in widening participation; the achievement of sector leadership in the promotion of creativity and innovation; and the conduct of business according to core values and the highest standards of corporate governance. The overall Plan was underpinned by annual business plans and targets, and by a regularly updated Corporate Risk Register. Under Vice-Chancellor Richard Barnett, Ulster's vision was 'to be a university with a national and international reputation for excellence, innovation and regional engagement'.[16]

16 *University of Ulster, Corporate Plan 2006–07 to 2010–11*, v.

Like all universities there were local, regional, national and international facets of its manifold activities. The last of these should not be underestimated: by 2005–6, for example, the University had 115,000 alumni in 116 countries worldwide. Yet its very title commanded that regional engagement remained an overriding priority, with successful partnerships within the province being a chief means of achieving its goals. The advent of a new, devolved administration in Northern Ireland in 2007 confirmed these imperatives. Devolution also opened up the possibility of a review of one of the constraints on the University's endeavours – the long-standing cap on numbers of full-time home and EU students. While few advocated a return to unrestricted growth, there was widespread cross-party support for such a review, together with a conviction that, in all the elaborations of government policy during previous decades, part-time students had been almost uniformly neglected. Ten years on from his Report, echoing one of Sir Derek Birley's convictions, Lord Dearing regretted that 'we didn't do more to address the needs of the part-time learner'.[17] In its pursuit of an ever stronger regional and community role, the University of Ulster wished to become a powerhouse contributing to the advancement of every aspect of human capability in Northern Ireland. As a twenty-first century University, it would work to be a crucible in which a post-conflict community could be helped to face the personal and occupational challenges of a knowledge society.

To return to our starting-point, the prognostications of both Sir Peter Swinnerton-Dyer and Sir Derek Birley in the early 1990s were largely borne out by events. The entire higher education sector in the United Kingdom, not just the University of Ulster, witnessed unprecedented growth and change during the ensuing period and all institutions had to be quick-witted and enterprising in pursuit of their objectives. While it did not welcome certain changes – notably those affecting student finances – and lamented slow progress in others, particularly the fuller integration of further and higher education in Northern Ireland, the University progressively modernised its operations, especially those supporting students, and continued to work to reforming agendas. In key respects it remained distinctive: in the nature and range of its courses; in its strong commitment to research-led knowledge and technology transfer; in the single-mindedness with which it prioritised its regional responsibilities; and, above all, in the size and composition of its student body. As it looked to the future, it remained a university 'with a difference'.

17 *Education Guardian*, 24 July 2007, 2.

7

The University in a Divided Society

THOMAS G. FRASER

'No man is an island, entire of itself'[1]

Throughout the years of violence and civil unrest in Northern Ireland, the University of Ulster, together with other educational institutions, made a distinctive, but vital, contribution to a society which often seemed hopelessly at odds with itself. Respecting the right of individuals to hold and express political views, the University strove to ensure that its campuses were 'neutral spaces' where students and staff could study and work in an atmosphere free from threat or discrimination. In doing so, it helped ensure that these were places where members of the two communities could meet in an atmosphere of mutual respect. But in a conflict which claimed over 3,500 lives, and in which many thousands more were injured, bereaved, or had their hopes frustrated and fears confirmed, it could not be expected that the institution would enjoy total immunity from the conflict which was going on around it. On Saturday 5 October 1968, as the first students of the New University of Ulster were about to embark upon their studies, Northern Ireland was thrust into the world's headlines when the Royal Ulster Constabulary attempted to disperse a march by civil rights protestors which had assembled in defiance of a government ban in Londonderry's Waterside. As rioting spread to other parts of the city, and television coverage flashed across the world, the history of Northern Ireland was changed for ever.

THE UNIVERSITY AND THE CONFLICT

While many events across three decades stirred emotions in the academic community, direct violence struck the institution on several

1 John Donne, 'Devotions upon Emergent Occasions, Meditation XVII' (1624).

occasions. On 4 November 1983, with the new institution then in the process of formation, a bomb in a lecture theatre at Jordanstown killed three policemen and caused many other injuries; it was not the first bomb attack on the campus, nor was it to be the last in the University. A prison education worker and two policemen were killed on the Magee campus on 23 March 1987. Ten years before, there had been a small device at Coleraine on the occasion of the royal visit to the New University. On at least two other occasions, the University was the setting for political interventions. On 16 December 1992, the Secretary of State for Northern Ireland, Sir Patrick Mayhew, made a highly significant speech on the Coleraine campus on the theme of 'Culture and Identity'. Then, in the aftermath of the Good Friday Agreement, on 20 May 1998 Prime Minister Tony Blair chose the Coleraine campus to emphasise key pledges on the part of the British government in advance of the Referendum which was about to be held. While the University of Ulster was cutting its distinctive niche in the history of higher education, in common with Queen's University in Belfast it was having to do so in an environment radically different to anything experienced by universities in Great Britain or the Republic of Ireland. How the University rose to the challenges of these years is an essential part of its history.

Individuals responded to events in different ways. Some chose, in a personal capacity, to take an active part in political life. A few acquired enviable reputations as commentators on political events in the press and on radio and television, their views listened to with respect for the fair-minded and lucid way they dealt with the affairs of a deeply divided community. Others became involved in the work of government commissions or with the non-departmental public bodies, which helped sustain public involvement in the affairs of Northern Ireland through the decades of direct rule from Westminster. Such commitment to the future well-being of Northern Ireland was never lacking, often through times when optimism was hard to find.

Since the conflict in Northern Ireland seemed stubbornly resistant to resolution, it was inevitable that it would become the focus of intense academic scrutiny. No other community in contemporary western Europe was undergoing such turmoil. Why was this? What were the issues? How were people affected? How might the conflict be resolved? Were there lessons that could be learned from, or applied in, other situations, such as the Middle East, South Africa, or Sri Lanka? These beguilingly simple questions held no easy answers, but academics made it their business to help find them and, as a result, Northern Ireland became one of the most studied societies in the world. University of Ulster scholars took their full part, with colleagues, chiefly in the arts, social sciences, psychology, and economics, well to the fore in the academic discourse of the time. Just as important was the impressive number of postgraduate theses on topics related to the social and economic structure, as well as the politics and contemporary history, of Northern Ireland, testimony both to the sense of engagement of their authors, and of the concern of their supervisors.

THE CENTRE FOR THE STUDY OF CONFLICT AND THE UNESCO CENTRE

By the late 1970s the conflict seemed to have developed its own momentum, with no sign of a political solution in the immediate future, in a society which had drawn apart into conflicting enclaves as a result of what was happening. In these rather bleak circumstances, a group of academics in the arts and social sciences came together in 1977 to establish the Centre for the Study of Conflict as an interdisciplinary research unit with a central focus on the conflict in Ireland. That year saw its first publication, *Education and Community in Northern Ireland: Schools Apart?* Given the University's academic strength in the area of Education, and the subject's importance for understanding the workings of society in Northern Ireland, it is not surprising that educational research formed a major part of the Centre's work over the years. The foundation of the religiously integrated Lagan College in Belfast in 1981 introduced a new dimension into an educational sector hitherto divided between the controlled and maintained sectors. A series of reports, including *Integrated Schools: Information for Parents* (1989), and *Breaking the Mould: The Roles of Parents and Teachers in the Integrated Schools in Northern Ireland* (1992) analysed this new element in educational provision. Several of these themes, including integrated education and the teaching of history in divided societies, were subsequently taken up by the UNESCO Centre. This was inaugurated on the Coleraine campus in February 2001 by Koichiro Matsuura, Director-General of UNESCO, and the Northern Ireland Minister for Further and Higher Education, Dr Sean Farren, who had himself made a distinguished contribution to the study of education at the University.

If educational issues were an obvious concern, over the period of the Centre's history, from 1977 to 2000, a varied series of externally funded research projects, and their associated published reports, informed thinking about how Northern Ireland was developing. Amongst the topics examined were *The Churches and Inter-Community Relationships* (1991), *Women, Community and Organisations* (1994), *Ethnic Residential Segregation in Belfast* (1995), *Policing a Divided Society* (1995), *Sport and Community Relations in Northern Ireland* (1995), *Disability and Religion in Northern Ireland* (1995), *Ethnic Minorities in Northern Ireland* (1996), and *Mixed Marriages in Northern Ireland* (1996). In 1994, as the paramilitary ceasefires were declared, the Centre addressed the issue next likely to generate conflict; namely, parading disputes. In June 1995, *Political Rituals: Loyalist Parades in Portadown* was published, which anticipated the turmoil which was to break out in the town only weeks later over the Drumcree church parade. This triggered an intensive study of parading disputes in Portadown, Belfast, Derry and other flashpoints over the next three years. *Parade and Protest: A Discussion of Parading Disputes in Northern Ireland* (1996) was a seminal analysis of the events which convulsed Northern Ireland in that year. Both these reports were cited in Dr Peter North's *Independent Review of Parades and Marches* (1997). They influenced and informed discussion of these contentious events. The reports of the Centre remain an essential source for anyone wishing to probe the complexities of Northern Irish society during these critical years, many of them remaining accessible through the CAIN website.

INCORE (INTERNATIONAL CONFLICT RESEARCH) AND ARK (ACCESS, RESEARCH, KNOWLEDGE)

In the early 1990s, the University sought to build upon the well-established reputation and wealth of expertise established by its researchers, notably by the Centre for the Study of Conflict. Such work deserved to be better known at the international level. It was also the right time for a new initiative. Violence in Northern Ireland continued at a high level, but the moves which were to culminate in the ceasefires of 1994 were under way. South Africa was in transformation. The Oslo Accords of 1993 seemed to offer a way forward in the interminable Arab–Israeli conflict, though this proved to be a

39 Dr Boutros Boutros Ghali, UN Secretary-General when UU and the
United Nations University established INCORE.

false dawn. The collapse of the Soviet Union and of communist
regimes across eastern Europe removed the threat of nuclear
holocaust, but opened a Pandora's box of long-suppressed ethnic
tensions. The Balkans were about to ignite. Conflict in Sri Lanka and
the perennial tensions between India and Pakistan over Kashmir
threatened the stability of south Asia. Research into conflict, and
conflict resolution, was never more important, and there was no more
appropriate location to carry it out than Northern Ireland.

An obvious partner in this enterprise was the United Nations
University (UNU). Established by the General Assembly of the
United Nations in 1973, the UNU had a particular brief with regard
to the international community of scholars, to act as a bridge between
the United Nations and the international academic community, to be
a think-tank for the United Nations, and to build capacities, especially

40 In 1997 the Crown Prince of Jordan, HRH El Hassan Bin Talal, visited INCORE for discussions on conflict resolution and was awarded an hononary doctorate.

in developing countries. In the summer of 1991 representatives of the University and the UNU began discussions for a feasibility study, and this was followed by the formation of an International Planning Study Group, including members from India, Mexico, Russia and the Republic of Ireland, to discuss research and training needs in conflict resolution and ethnicity. Their discussions resulted in the proposal to establish the Joint International Programme on Conflict Resolution and Ethnicity. Known by the acronym INCORE, the title was later shortened to International Conflict Research. In November 1992, the Vice-Chancellor, Professor Trevor Smith, and the Rector of the UNU signed a Memorandum of Agreement, and this was followed in January 1993 by the ratification by the UNU's Council of INCORE's status as an affiliated centre.

41 UN official Cedric Thornberry (*centre*), first holder of the Tip O'Neill
Visiting Chair in Peace Studies.

Although priorities were to change over time, INCORE's initial
objective was the encouragement of the understanding of ethnic
conflict and of approaches to conflict resolution. It hoped to do this
through high quality research; training in conflict resolution and
management; fostering interactions between research, training, policy,
practice and theory; and, through its research and training, informing
and influencing national and international organisations working in
the area of ethnic conflict. Through time INCORE developed its
policy and practice work, building relationships between academia and
practitioners, and sharing lessons from Northern Ireland with other
parts of the world which were having to address similar issues and
challenges. Such an ambitious agenda required funding, essential
initial support coming from, amongst other sources, the Department
of Education for Northern Ireland in the form of NIDevR funds, the
Central Community Relations Unit and the European Union. An
important milestone was reached in September 1995 when a special
graduation ceremony, marking both the fiftieth anniversary of the
United Nations Organization and INCORE's move to the Magee
campus, was held in Derry's Guildhall to honour former UN Secretary-
General Xavier Perez de Cuellar and Lucille Mair, Chairperson of the

UNU Council. INCORE's base was to be Aberfoyle House, a fine Victorian mansion, owned in the nineteenth century by the McCorkell family whose shipping line had been so much part of the city's history. INCORE was officially opened in June 1996 by Lieutenant-General Satish Nambiar, who had taken a leading role in peacekeeping in the former Yugoslavia. A notable feature of INCORE's activities was its annual summer school, which addressed both theoretical and practical dimensions to peacebuilding in the context of Northern Ireland. The 2007 summer school attracted 50 participants from Afghanistan, Belgium, Bosnia-Herzegovina, Canada, Colombia, England, Germany, Ireland, Israel, Italy, Kenya, Monrovia, Northern Ireland, Norway, Senegal, Sierra Leone, Slovakia, Spain, Tchad, the Netherlands, Uganda and the United States, testimony to INCORE's international reputation as well as to a continuing interest in pursuing the progress of a society coming out of conflict.

An important collaboration between the University and Queen's University Belfast was ARK (Access, Research, Knowledge). From its University of Ulster base within INCORE, ARK has provided an invaluable resource for schools, journalists, policymakers, and indeed anyone with an interest in analysing and tracing the changing political and social attitudes of the Northern Ireland public. These may be monitored through the annual *Northern Ireland Life and Times Survey*, established in 1998, and its partner, the *Young Life and Times Survey*. An example of the *Survey*'s sensitivity to the changing nature of society in Northern Ireland was the inclusion in 2006 of a section on 'Attitudes to Minority Ethnic People'.

THE TIP O'NEILL CHAIR IN PEACE STUDIES

In the years that followed, INCORE and the University continued to attract international visitors of the highest calibre, sharing their experiences of peacemaking. In May 1996 the Secretary-General of the Commonwealth, Chief Emeka Anyaoku, visited Magee and spoke on preventative diplomacy, while the following December Crown Prince Hassan of Jordan lectured on his role in the Middle East peace process on the occasion of receiving an honorary degree at Jordanstown. Of particular significance was the creation of the Tip O'Neill Chair in Peace Studies in memory of the former Speaker of the House of Representatives whose forebears had come from Inishowen. This was inaugurated by President Bill Clinton during his historic visit to Derry in December 1995, the first lecture under its auspices being delivered by Senator Edward M. Kennedy in the Guildhall on 9 January 1998 on 'Northern Ireland: A View from America'.

The first two holders of the Tip O'Neill Chair were Deputy Secretary-General of the United Nations Cedric Thornberry and Rolf Meyer, a leading figure in the South African peace negotiations. In November 2002 the Chair was taken up by John Hume, who had recently stepped down as leader of the Social Democratic and Labour Party, and who had been joint recipient of the Nobel Peace Prize in 1998. As the result of his invitations, and funded by The Ireland Funds, the Magee campus witnessed a succession of world figures who spoke on the subject of peace and peacemaking: former French premier Michel Rocard; former President Bill Clinton; An Taoiseach Bertie Ahern, while President of the European Council; the President of the European Commission, Professor Romano Prodi; the President of the European Parliament, Pat Cox; Senator Hillary Rodham Clinton; the Secretary-General of the United Nations, Kofi Annan; former Taoiseach Dr Garret FitzGerald; Senator John Kerry; Ambassador Mitchell Reiss; President Mary McAleese; Irish Minister for Foreign Affairs, Dermot Ahern; Dr Maurice Hayes, former Head of the Northern Ireland Civil Service; and former South African Minister of Education, Professor Kader Asmal. They shared a wealth of experience with capacity audiences drawn from both the local and academic communities.

CAIN (CONFLICT ARCHIVE ON THE INTERNET)

A further initiative was launched in 1995. This was the Conflict Archive on the INternet (CAIN), initially a joint project with Queen's University and the Linenhall Library in Belfast, though subsequently entirely based in the University of Ulster. Its purpose was very simple, though technologically demanding. It was to make available through the internet research materials on the conflict, which researchers, especially overseas, would otherwise find difficulty in accessing. CAIN was to produce a comprehensive archive relating to the key events and issues of the conflict, so that, for example, a researcher in Bremen or Brisbane who needed information on Northern Ireland politics would find *inter alia* a selected reading list, details of the local councils, an outline of the main political initiatives, a guide to the political parties, a summary of election results from 1968, a selection of party manifestos, electoral charts and maps, and details of constituencies. In October 2006 CAIN embarked on a new project, funded by the Arts and Humanities Research Council, to produce a comprehensive archive relating to victims and commemorations in post-conflict Northern Ireland. It is doubtful if any conflict has been as comprehensively documented, and as the number of people across the world with access to the internet increased, it is not surprising that by 2007 CAIN had registered over 45 million 'hits'.

COMING OUT OF CONFLICT

It could not be said that the issues generated by the conflict were ignored in teaching, since Irish history or politics featured in various programmes at Coleraine, Jordanstown and Magee. When arts teaching was restored at Magee after the merger, a distinctive new feature was the area of Peace Studies. While the undergraduate provision in Peace Studies was phased out in time, at the postgraduate level it went from strength to strength. As the Postgraduate/MA in Peace and Conflict Studies, its syllabus featured Peace and Conflict Studies Research, International Conflict and Cooperation, the Politics of Divided Societies, and the Northern Ireland Conflict. This mixture of the local with the global dimensions to conflict attracted students from across the world, including Brazil, Canada, Germany, Japan, Sweden, the United States, as well as from Northern Ireland.

The 1998 Agreement did not confine itself to political and constitutional issues. It included broader provisions about the future of Northern Irish society, some of which were reflected in the University's activities, although it need hardly be said that the University was not a party to this, or any other, political settlement. As part of its cultural provision, the Irish language was to be promoted. The University had long enjoyed a strong reputation for teaching and research in Irish, and this was confirmed in 2001 when Celtic Studies was awarded a 5* rating, the highest possible score, in the United Kingdom-wide Research Assessment Exercise, and the subject gained a 24 rating, again the highest possible, in the assessment of teaching. In response to demand, Irish language provision was expanded from

42 Façade of Aberfoyle House, Magee campus.

its existing base on the Coleraine campus, with part-time degree programmes being established at Belfast in 2001 and Magee in 2003. The Diploma in Irish was another significant 'gateway' into the language for both Northern Ireland and the Republic of Ireland. As the result of this expansion, the University became the largest provider of Irish in further and higher education in Northern Ireland. The Agreement also recognised the importance of Ulster Scots. 2001 saw the establishment on the Magee campus of the Institute of Ulster Scots Studies, funded by a grant from the Ulster Scots Agency, which had as its brief the promotion of the understanding of Ulster Scots history, culture and heritage within Ulster and beyond to those regions where the Ulster Scots had influenced the development of specific communities and nations. The Institute developed a wide-ranging research agenda in the areas of history and cultural heritage, which it promoted in a variety of ways, including its book series 'Ulster and Scotland'. An interesting example of community outreach was its participation in the 'Women into Irish History' project, which brought together a group of Protestant and Catholic women in Derry to foster an understanding of what they termed their Shared City.

The future of policing was addressed by a committee under former Hong Kong governor, Chris Patten, who was given an honorary doctorate by the University in 2005 for his contribution to public life and education. The Patten Committee reported in September 1999, as a result of which the Police Service of Northern Ireland (PSNI) came into being in November 2001. On successful completion of their initial training programme, police recruits were awarded the University of Ulster's Certificate in Police Studies, an exemplar of its kind in police education. This continued a long-standing commitment to police education, which began in 1973 when the Ulster Polytechnic introduced a part-time Higher National Certificate in Police Studies. Its alumni included five Assistant Chief Constables and a Chief Constable.

Human rights was also a key issue for Northern Ireland. In June 2005 the University's Institute of Transitional Justice, based at Jordanstown and Magee, was opened by Justice Albie Sachs, one of the legendary figures in the struggle against the injustices of apartheid in South Africa. While the conventional view of transitional justice was that of confronting the legal, moral and political dilemmas arising from human rights abuses in societies coming out of conflict, the Transitional Justice Institute sought to examine more broadly how the law and legal institutions might assist the move from conflict to peace.

If we accept John Donne's meditation, then we can see how this institution responded to, and was affected by, what was happening in Northern Ireland through the long years of civil conflict. Although violence did impinge upon it, it remained an island of calm where students could pursue their hopes for a better future for themselves and their society. But the University did engage with the issues of that society with all the academic rigour and integrity at its command. Its record is there, in the public domain, and there it will be judged, now and in the future.

Appendix

Table 1: Student Numbers 1984/5–2005/6

	1984/85	1985/86	1986/87	1987/88	1988/89	1989/90	1990/91	1991/92	1992/93	1993/94	1994/95
JORDANSTOWN											
Full-time	4,758	4,409	4,395	4,485	4,609	4,685	4,730	5,099	5,485	5,921	6,077
Part-time	2,910	2,831	2,680	2,714	2,882	2,996	3,240	3,489	3,827	4,061	4,324
Jordanstown total	7,668	7,240	7,075	7,199	7,491	7,681	7,970	8,588	9,312	9,982	10,401
COLERAINE											
Full-time	2,148	2,235	2,324	2,461	2,380	2,511	2,917	3,156	3,638	4,136	4,180
Part-time	283	329	311	330	331	422	467	556	578	589	625
Coleraine total	2,431	2,564	2,635	2,791	2,711	2,933	3,384	3,712	4,216	4,725	4,805
BELFAST											
Full-time	380	540	532	560	624	653	689	717	692	765	849
Part-time	177	133	115	112	54	33	16	25	30	42	38
Belfast total	557	673	647	672	678	686	705	742	722	807	887
MAGEE											
Full-time	172	276	362	462	683	786	869	1,014	1,156	1,342	1,438
Part-time	354	452	506	514	570	630	685	771	838	919	1,067
Magee total	526	728	868	976	1,253	1,416	1,554	1,785	1,994	2,261	2,505
Total by mode											
Full-time	7,458	7,460	7,613	7,968	8,296	8,635	9,205	9,986	10,971	12,164	12,544
Part-time	3,724	3,745	3,612	3,670	3,837	4,081	4,408	4,841	5,273	5,611	6,054
University total	11,182	11,205	11,225	11,638	12,133	12,716	13,613	14,827	16,244	17,775	18,598

	1995/96	1996/97	1997/98	1998/99	1999/00	2000/01	2001/02	2002/03	2003/04	2004/05	2005/06
JORDANSTOWN											
Full-time	6,637	6,404	6,500	6,621	6,786	7,287	7,798	8,328	8,584	8,908	8,785
Part-time	4,818	4,986	5,180	5,185	5,123	4,950	4,513	4,697	5,309	5,339	5,290
Jordanstown total	11,455	11,390	11,680	11,806	11,909	12,237	12,311	13,025	13,893	14,247	14,075
COLERAINE											
Full-time	4,397	4,124	4,005	4,029	4,044	4,104	3,919	4,144	4,223	4,130	4,349
Part-time	574	511	516	583	727	864	1,012	1,044	1,464	1,143	1,175
Coleraine total	4,971	4,635	4,521	4,612	4,771	4,968	4,931	5,188	5,687	5,273	5,524
BELFAST											
Full-time	934	877	907	874	890	911	908	923	1,045	890	1,007
Part-time	35	41	36	33	87	126	146	181	168	182	181
Belfast total	969	918	943	907	977	1,037	1,054	1,104	1,213	1,072	1,188
MAGEE											
Full-time	1,580	1,638	1,719	1,754	1,892	1,907	2,064	2,559	2,645	2,893	2,980
Part-time	1,067	1,030	1,080	1,053	1,106	1,024	860	836	806	904	887
Magee total	2,647	2,668	2,799	2,807	2,998	2,931	2,924	3,395	3,451	3,797	3,867
Total by mode											
Full-time	13,548	13,043	13,131	13,278	13,612	14,209	14,689	15,954	16,497	16,821	17,121
Part-time	6,494	6,568	6,812	6,854	7,043	6,964	6,531	6,758	7,747	7,568	7,533
University total	20,042	19,611	19,943	20,132	20,655	21,173	21,220	22,712	24,244	24,389	24,654

Table 2: Students Enrolled on Validated Courses at Recognised Institutions 1992/3–2005/6

	1992/93	1993/94	1994/95	1995/96	1996/97	1997/98	1998/99	1999/00
HND	382	402	590	693	625	701	785	877
HNC	82	90	138	177	395	488	545	596
Other	2,173	2,667	3,046	3,360	3,013	1,775	2,295	2,497
University total	2,637	3,159	3,774	4,230	4,033	2,964	3,625	3,970

	2000/01	2001/02	2002/03	2003/04	2004/05	2005/06
HND	861	790	554	479	355	312
HNC	607	541	575	498	330	289
Other	2,748	3,597	3,959	4,588	4,438	4,243
University total	4,216	4,928	5,088	5,565	5,123	4,844

Table 3: Student Numbers by Gender 1984/5–2005/6

	1984/85	1985/86	1986/87	1987/88	1988/89	1989/90	1990/91	1991/92	1992/93	1993/94	1994/95
MALE											
Full-time	3,848	3,823	3,797	3,868	3,900	3,982	4,160	4,459	4,850	5,355	5,493
Part-time	2,602	2,517	2,293	2,257	2,234	2,323	2,446	2,620	2,827	2,956	3,131
Male total	6,450	6,340	6,090	6,125	6,134	6,305	6,606	7,079	7,677	8,311	8,624
FEMALE											
Full-time	3,610	3,637	3,816	4,100	4,396	4,653	5,045	5,527	6,121	6,809	7,051
Part-time	1,122	1,228	1,319	1,413	1,603	1,758	1,962	2,221	2,446	2,655	2,923
Female total	4,732	4,865	5,135	5,513	5,999	6,411	7,007	7,748	8,567	9,464	9,974
University total	11,182	11,205	11,225	11,638	12,133	12,716	13,613	14,827	16,244	17,775	18,598

	1995/96	1996/97	1997/98	1998/99	1999/00	2000/01	2001/02	2002/03	2003/04	2004/05	2005/06
MALE											
Full-time	5,951	5,608	5,528	5,509	5,600	5,822	5,987	6,348	6,903	6,767	7,046
Part-time	3,250	3,153	2,989	2,812	2,857	2,771	2,511	2,451	2,626	2,785	2,855
Male total	9,201	8,761	8,517	8,321	8,457	8,593	8,498	8,799	9,529	9,552	9,901
FEMALE											
Full-time	7,597	7,435	7,603	7,769	8,012	8,387	8,702	9,606	10,203	10,054	10,075
Part-time	3,244	3,415	3,823	4,042	4,186	4,193	4,020	4,307	4,512	4,783	4,678
Female total	10,841	10,850	11,426	11,811	12,198	12,580	12,722	13,913	14,715	14,837	14,753
University total	20,042	19,611	19,943	20,132	20,655	21,173	21,220	22,712	24,244	24,389	24,654

Index